Oliver Skroch

Developing Business Application Systems

GABLER RESEARCH

Oliver Skroch

Developing Business Application Systems

On the Specification and Selection of Software Components and Services

GABLER

RESEARCH

Bibliographic information published by the Deutsche Nationalbibliothek
The Deutsche Nationalbibliothek lists this publication in the Deutsche Nationalbibliografie;
detailed bibliographic data are available in the Internet at http://dnb.d-nb.de.

Dissertation Universität Augsburg, 2009

1st Edition 2010

Editorial Office: Ute Wrasmann | Britta Göhrisch-Radmacher

Gabler Verlag is a brand of Springer Fachmedien.
Springer Fachmedien is part of Springer Science+Business Media.
www.gabler.de

Umschlaggestaltung: KünkelLopka Medienentwicklung, Heidelberg
Printed on acid-free paper

ISBN 978-3-8349-2350-9

Preface

The urge for a better, cheaper, and faster development and tailoring of application software systems can be explained by their high importance: well-working information processing is a required precondition for the prosperity – or even for the mere survival – of many businesses and institutions. Hence it is a highly warrantable and topical objective to significantly improve software development by new technologies and methods, to increase quality and benefits while at the same time decreasing lifecycle costs and project durations. Where, however, are reasonable starting points for research activities that pursue these objectives? Software reuse and in particular the closely related component- and service-orientation are among the few fundamental approaches that show greatest promise. This book presents six respective research articles.

The book is based on my cumulative doctoral thesis and I feel indebted to many people and their support. I thank Prof. Dr. Klaus Turowski in the first place. He enabled my integration as an external researcher at the Chair of Business Informatics and Systems Engineering, Universität Augsburg, and he provided most valuable support in decisive situations. I give my thanks to Prof. Dr. Robert Klein for the second opinion on my dissertation and to Prof. Dr. Axel Tuma for presiding the disputation. I am grateful to my co-authors Dr. Sven Overhage and Michael Pruß for the good, successful, and pleasant team work on our research articles.

Finally, I am happy to acknowledge the support of many good and unnamed spirits both in my private and professional world. You were always able to show understanding for my research and you tolerated the vast amount of time and effort that I dedicated to science – you only came second so often and although you have deserved to come first just as well.

Augsburg, February 2010   Oliver Skroch

Contents

List of figures

List of tables

Abbreviations

AHP	Analytic Hierarchy Process
aka	also known as
ARIval	Abstraction, Reduction, Inclusion and Validation
avg.	average
BGH	Bundesgerichtshof (Federal Court of Justice, Germany)
BSS	Business Support System
BU	Business Unit
CAPEX	Capital Expenditure
CC	Call Center
COTS	Commercial Off-The-Shelf
CR	Customer Representative
CRM	Customer Relationship Management
CUA	Cost-Utility Analysis
doi	digital object identifier
DSP	Digital Signal Processing
DP	Data Processing
DW	Data Warehouse
dept.	department
e. g.	exempli gratia
EPC	Event-driven Process Chain
exp.	experiment
GoBS	Grundsätze ordnungsmäßiger DV-gestützter Buchführungssysteme (statutory regulations for electronic accounting systems in Germany)
ICT	Information and Communication Technology
IDE	integrated development environment
IN	Intelligent Network
IP	Internet Protocol
IS	Information System
ITU	International Telecommunication Union
ITU-T	ITU – Telecommunication Standardization Sector
MIS	Management Information System
NGN	Next Generation Network
OCL	Object Constraint Language
OMG	Object Management Group
OSS	Operations Support System
P1 to P9	phases from the multi-path process model
PDP-6	Programmed Data Processor 6

QoS	Quality of Service
SEAA	Software Engineering and Advanced Applications
SIG	Special Interest Group
spec.	specification
TCO	Total Cost of Ownership
TTCN	Testing and Test Control Notation
UDDI	Universal Description, Discovery and Integration
UK	United Kingdom
UML	Unified Modeling Language
UnSCom	Unified Specification of Components
val.	validation
ver.	verification
VoIP	Voice over IP
Z	Zermelo-Fraenkel notation

Symbols

$\rightarrow$	converges to
$\emptyset$	empty set
∞	infinity
$>>$	much greater than
$\approx$	approximately equal
A	σ-algebra
E	expected value
e	Euler's number
ε	arbitrarily small positive quantity
F	distribution function
I	indicator function
inf	infimum
ln	natural logarithm
max	maximum
O	Landau notation
Ω	set of all elementary events (sample space)
P	probability measure
sup	supremum
σ	sigma-operator
T	class of stopping rules
τ	stopping rule

I   Introduction

I.1   Motivation and challenges

"Better! Cheaper! Faster!" is a battle cry in today's economy that sounds across many lines of businesses, from the investors' desks through executive management levels down to operational projects (Brandon 2006, p. 4). The three cardinal challenges of this objective are depicted in the structure of the "triple constraint" triangle illustrated in Figure I-1 (Rosenau 1981, pp. 15-18). Some difficulties, however, arise from the dynamics of the "triple constraint", from the challenges associated with achieving all three dependent conditions simultaneously: "Unfortunately, the Triple Constraint is very difficult to satisfy because most of what occurs during a project conspires to pull the performance below specification and to delay the project so it falls behind schedule, which makes it exceed the budget." (Rosenau 1981, p. 15).

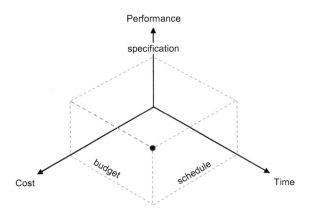

Figure I-1: "Triple Constraint". Cf. Rosenau (1981, p. 16).

While the "triple constraint" explicates important aspects of the desire for better, cheaper, and faster results, the ambition itself has reached IT development processes first among others (Voas 2001, p. 96; Brandon 2006, pp. 4-6). This can be explained by the high importance of IT in businesses and administrations. The so-called "business-IT alignment" – a close and mutual calibration of business objectives and IT capabilities – has become a necessary prerequisite for competition and mere survival in many areas (Henderson & Venkatraman 1993, p. 476; Teubner 2006, pp. 368f).

Looking at IT as a whole, we can distinguish between hardware and software. It has attracted our attention for decades that the development of IT electronics and computing *hardware* achieves extreme improvements in performance which can also be predicted quite reliably.

Soon after the integrated circuit had been invented, Moore (1965, pp. 114-117) stated that the complexity of these integrated circuits will double every or every second year at minimum component costs. At that time, the opinion of the Intel co-founder Moore appeared too fantastic to be true. Today, it is considered to be verified and is often referred to as Moore's Law in the sense of a natural process.

In comparison, the development of *software* typically starts seemingly harmless and simple, only to disappoint expectations later – expectations which were set accordingly high by stakeholders benchmarking on hardware development. Software development is notorious for delivering poor results, exploding budgets, and missed milestones (Brooks 1987, p. 10; DeMarco 1997, pp. 1-6; Glass 2006, p. 15). When the costs for software exceeded the hardware costs for the first time in the 1960s, the term of a "software crisis" was coined. Since then software development has been exposed to a particular criticism: it does not achieve performance gains according to benchmarks set by the progress in electronics and computing hardware (Naur & Randell 1969, pp. 13f, pp. 65ff; Dijkstra 1972, p. 866). Apart from technical causes also reasons rooting in the planning and organizing of software development have been discussed (Martin & Chang 1994, pp. 14f; Glass 1996, pp. 183f). Chatzoglou (1997, p. 627), for instance, underlines the "inadequate project management caused by a lack of recognising and understanding what the real problems are in carrying out software development."

Consequently, the desire for new technologies and management methods has emerged, with the intention to stipulate significant improvements in the development of software and to achieve productivity gains similar to the benchmarks from hardware development.

The three most significant performance improvements in the history of software development are described by Brooks (1987, pp. 12f). By introducing *higher programming languages* in the 1950s ("Fortran" from IBM), problems from the physical construction of a computer were eliminated. Higher programming languages abstract software from the basic properties of a computing machine, such as bit endians or registers. They pass for the greatest progress made by now. By introducing *multi user systems* in the 1960s ("PDP-6" from DEC), problems from the exclusive and sequential use of a computer were eliminated. Several developers could work "in parallel" via terminals on one computer and could compile and execute their code on their own. By introducing *integrated development environments (IDEs)* in the 1970s ("Interlisp" from Xerox), problems from the integration of different tools into a tool chain were eliminated. Developers had a predefined environment in which the source code was transformed into executable software. Their "workbenches" included, for instance, editor, library functions, compiler, linker, binder, and debugger.

In this context, object-orientation (Dahl & Nygaard 1966; Meyer 1990; Rumbaugh et al. 1993) is an often discussed concept. Object-orientation allows to represent software on a higher abstraction level. It is an important advantage that the additional, object-oriented abstraction concepts enforce an even more systematic development. On the other hand, object-orientation does not simplify the development, and the essential challenges in developing software are not rooted in the representation of a solution, but in the solution itself. Object-oriented methods, therefore, have not generated significant performance improvements (Brooks 1987, p. 14; Potok, Vouk & Rindos 1999, p. 844; Glass 2005, p. 18).

The greatest productivity gains in software development have so far been related quite closely to the implementation, and have considerably contributed to recognizing more clearly the ensuing difficulties which are part of the character and essence of the discipline (Brooks 1987, pp. 11f):

- *Extreme complexity*. No two parts are equal in software above the source code level. If they are, they are realized as the same component, the same object, the same module, the same function and so on. In this way, software systems differ profoundly from other existing systems. Moreover, software can take extremely many states. A software system with 300 binary variables is regarded as small, but it can take 2^{300} ($\approx 10^{90}$) states. These are about one hundred billion times more system states than the number of atoms in the observable universe, which is estimated in the range of 10^{79} today (Wikipedia 2009).

- *Arbitrary conformance*. Software systems, and in particular application systems in business and administration, must conform to other human-made institutions, systems, products etc. at their interfaces. These are arbitrarily defined cultural artifacts that do not always follow universal rules and laws that can be explained rationally. This is an important difference to physics, for instance, where high complexity is an issue, too. However, when analyzing "the other side of the interfaces" physics has an easier task because it encounters unchanging laws of nature.

- *Constant changeability*. In remarkable contrast to other technical systems, software is regularly changed fundamentally also after having been placed into live operation. Although the related high efforts and risks are understood and respected when changing finalized and operating technical products in other domains, for instance, building reconstructions, changing live software is deemed to be comparatively easy. One reason might be that software is intangible, not physically touchable, and thus defies an intuitive comprehension.

- *Invisibility*. Software systems cannot be visualized properly, because no simple spatial correspondent is known for the reality of software. Visualization approaches, as well as description models without graphical notation, lead to multi-dimensional, mutually depending levels of descriptions and diagrams. They raise challenging questions as to the dependencies and relations between the specified levels and the facts. Cf., for instance, Overhage (2006, pp. 125-129) for further reading.

Essential difficulties in developing software go beyond its implementation. Parnas (1985, pp. 1327f) describes fundamental differences between software engineering and other engineering disciplines, and exposes reasons why software is unreliable in principle. The argument starts from the basic difference between analog and discrete systems.

Analog systems have infinitely many states (examples include speakers, motors, or radiators). Their behavior can be described adequately using continuous functions. Such systems are items of traditional engineering domains, and the related mathematics of continuous functions is well understood. Within their operating range, analog systems cannot contain any "hidden surprises": small input changes always cause correspondingly small output changes. Hence, reliable behavior of analog systems can be guaranteed by mathematical analysis and description within the operating range, and by testing to ensure that the system operates within the defined range. *Discrete systems* have a finite number of stable states. Their behavior outside of the defined stable states is irrelevant. The earliest discrete systems, before the modern computer, had so few states that they could be tested exhaustively and therefore were fully understood without an analytical description (one example is railway signaling control). The first discrete computer systems already had extremely many states, but were made up of identically repeating copies of few subsystem types. Therefore, they could be exhaustively tested and completely understood, too (an example is the semiconductor memory). *Hybrid systems* consist of components that have a small number of discrete states and, between the few different states, are described by continuous functions (one example is the diode).

A decisive implication for any system planning and development originates from the modeling of the system types. With analog systems, continuous mathematical functions are available, but they cannot be applied to discrete system. For software systems we see that:

- different from traditional analog technology, they are discrete, therefore they can not be described using continuous functions and the calculus – actually, there is no simple mathematical or logical description method known by now;

- different from computing hardware, their behavior can also not be mastered by full testing ("brute force"), because software systems have extremely many states and no repeating structure, so exhaustive testing is prevented by the related efforts.

Parnas (1985, p. 1328) recognizes these conditions as "fundamental difference that will not disappear with improved technology". They originate from the character of software and must be considered in the development of software applications, when defining strategic targets, when arranging tactical plans, and when realizing operational projects. Few fundamental approaches seem to appreciate these findings explicitly and thus clearly qualify for driving the development of application software significantly towards the "triple constraint" vision:

- *Education of experts* (Brooks 1987, p. 18; Parnas 1985, p. 1328; Wissenschaftliche Kommission Wirtschaftsinformatik 2003). Acting on the assumption that the differences between outstanding work and average work are roughly one decimal power (not only) in software development (Sackman, Erikson & Grant 1968, pp. 5f; Boehm 1986, p. 596), maybe the single most promising approach is to find, educate, support, and advance motivated and able experts.

- *Strategic software reuse* (Biggerstaff & Richter 1987; Mili, Mili & Mili 1995; Rost 1997). "Buy versus make" solution approaches aim at minimizing development tasks by reusing ready-made (partial) solutions that are already available wherever this is possible. One major challenge is the applicability of externally sourced components in the own, different context. Due to the lack of commonly accepted standards in software engineering, among other reasons, this applicability cannot simply be assumed today. Poulin (1997, p. 145) therefore states, "to achieve real results, we must institutionalize reuse", and Mili, Mili and Mili (1995, p. 529) even describe the concept of reuse as the only realistic solution path, "That leaves us with software reuse as the only realistic, technically feasible solution: We could reuse the processes and products of previous development efforts in order to develop new applications."

- *Component- and service-orientation*. These solution approaches are based on the "divide and conquer" principle. They aim at dividing a large task into ever smaller parts, until the small parts can be solved independently and can then be put together again to make up a large, loosely coupled overall solution. One major challenge is to find the right parts (components and services). In software engineering, this challenge is already known from structured analysis (module demarcation) or from object-orientation (object identification) and systematic, optimizing approaches are being discussed today. From the beginning, component- und service-oriented approaches have been closely interlocked with reuse concepts (Neighbors 1984, pp. 567f; Sametinger 1997, pp. 9ff, pp. 67ff). Component-orientation (Wassermann & Gutz 1982; Szyperski 1998; Brown 2000) and service-orientation (Schulte & Natis 1996; Schulte 1996; Atkinson et al. 2002; Fröschle & Reinheimer 2007) mainly differ in the reused item. Component-orientation reuses the components themselves; service-orientation reuses services that are implemented by the components.

Therefore, the book is motivated from the strategic framework of software reuse, by the expected advantages of a component- and service-oriented software development approach. In this context, the main part of the book presents research results that try to contribute to the progress in developing software application systems.

I.2   Objectives and focal research questions

Derived from the philosophy of science, the explanation and creation of the objects of investigation can be regarded as the main tasks in business informatics; in addition, the description and prediction can be named as supplementary tasks; particularly high significance is attached to the creative task (Mertens et al. 2005, pp. 4f; Heinrich, Heinzl & Roithmayr 2007, p. 21). The creative task builds upon description, explanation, and prediction, and aims at producing a desired target condition.

The objective of scientific investigations in business informatics can be described as producing findings, theories, methods, and tools for "people-task-technology" systems and infrastructures of information and communication in business and administration; the long-term goal is a reasonably full automation (Wissenschaftliche Kommission Wirtschaftsinfor-matik 1994, p. 81; Mertens et al. 2005, p. 4; Heinrich, Heinzl & Roithmayr 2007, p. 16, p. 21). In business informatics, contributions that are relevant for practical application and produce validated and verified findings are particularly desired and required (Wissenschaftliche Kommission Wirtschaftsinformatik 1994, p. 81).

The research articles that are presented in the main part of this book pursue creative goals with practical relevance. The contributions propose applicable scientific findings for the practical advancement of real software development, and thus for the improvement of the foundations for planning and realizing development tasks for application software systems. The following specific research goals have been pursued and the respective focal research questions examined:

Main part II, strategic framework, article R1: A theory of software reuse strategies in ideal type stable and turbulent market environments.

Reuse-driven software development exceeds the boundaries of traditional software development projects by explicitly incorporating global markets into its value creation chain, for example, in procurement and sales of reusable artifacts. Therefore, market conditions can be considered when framing long-term software reuse strategies. Research article R1 aims at supporting and advancing the strategic definition of software reuse approaches by proposing a theory of their preferences in ideal type market environments. The following focal research questions are explored:

• Which fundamental reuse approaches are known?

• Which ideal type market conditions can be distinguished with respect to reuse-driven application software development?

- Can strategic preferences be derived for certain reuse approaches from the market environments and if so, which?

Main part II, strategic framework, article R2: Integration assessment of an individually developed application vs. software packages from the market – an experience report.

With many and very specific requirements for a highly complex business application system, the basic decision in practice is often whether to either integrate the solution from prefabricated products that are available on the market or rather to develop an individual solution. Research article R2 aims at analyzing the strategy of individual development, as compared to the procurement and integration of business components from the market. Results from examinations in practical industry projects are presented and examined. The following focal research questions are explored:

- How well does an individually developed, large, and complex application system meet its requirements?

- How well by comparison are these same requirements met by a collection of software packages from the market?

- Can the analysis of several "make-or-buy" reference projects provide findings relevant for the general preference of individual development or procurement and if so, which?

Main part III, specification, article R3: The importance of requirements specifications for successful IT projects.

Specifying requirements belongs to the most critical activities in software development. It has always been a demanding challenge and gains a particularly central significance in modern, divided development work. Research article R3 aims at presenting success factors for the creation of high quality requirements specifications as derived from practical experience. These factors can be seen as foundations for a tactical planning. The research article also presents practical risks that can emerge from insufficient specifications. The following focal research questions are explored:

- What is the significance of requirements specifications in real software development practices?

- Which critical success factors can be identified that enable and improve the creation of high quality requirements specifications in software development projects?

- What practical consequences can result from deficient scope of work descriptions, especially with the division of software development work?

Main part III, specification, article R4: A method to evaluate the suitability of requirements specifications for offshore projects.

Today, globally divided application software development work typically includes offshore parts in design and programming. The quality of the underlying requirements specifications is especially important in such an offshore context. Research article R4 presents a method for the evaluation of requirements specifications as to the offshore assignment of downstream development steps, and employs the method in a large case study embedded into a real industry project. The following focal research questions are explored:

- How can requirements specifications be evaluated systematically for their suitability in downstream offshore development steps?
- Which courses of action can possibly be derived from the results of such an evaluation?
- What findings can be gained when actually performing such an evaluation in a real context?

Main part IV, selection, article R5: Optimal stopping for the run-time self-adaptation of software systems.

Already today, certain application systems ("mashups") use (Web-)services that are publicly available on the Internet. In doing so, service calls at run time are opportunistically delegated to services that are available on the open Internet. Choosing such an external service is an operational challenge, since there can be vast amounts of available service candidates and the Internet cannot be controlled. Research article R5 aims at improving the operational dynamic selection of reusable (Web-)services by means of applied mathematical statistics. The following focal research questions are explored:

- What circumstances characterize the dynamic opportunistic run-time search for suitable services on open platforms?
- Which assumptions must be made and which methods can be applied to improve the search and the selection under those circumstances?
- What advantages can be expected?

Main part IV, selection, article R6: Reducing domain level scenarios to test component-based software.

Contributions to software testing theory traditionally focus on formal and syntactical issues. Testing software for its semantic and pragmatic suitability in a business process – "higher-order" testing on the end-user side – has received comparatively little attention by now. This difficult operational challenge has high practical relevance though. Research article R6 aims at providing methodical support for selecting pragmatically suitable components and services by proposing a method for early specification checks against business process models. The following focal research questions are explored:

- How can it be checked if a software solution is suitable from the semantic and in particular from the pragmatic viewpoint, assuming an intended support and automation for an end-to-end business process?

- On what basis can such checks be carried out as early as possible in a reuse-driven software development cycle?

- How can complex business process models be reduced to serve as a starting point for the definition of "higher-order" test scenarios which can easily be interpreted?

I.3 Classification and organization

Different proposals for the segmentation of the business informatics discipline into research areas are being discussed today. Substantial segmentation proposals include, next to the philosophy of science-based approach, especially the business management-oriented approach and the approach with regard to contents (Heinrich, Heinzl & Roithmayr 2007, pp. 21f).

For the classification of this book's contributions, initially the approach with regard to contents is well-suited, since this approach strongly emphasizes creative research targets. On the one hand, the contents of the research articles presented in this book have a strong software engineering relation and therefore can be classified into the (reuse-driven) *development of application software systems*, which belongs to the central research topics in business informatics (Alpar et al. 2008, pp. 287ff; Ferstl & Sinz 2008, pp. 457ff; Heinrich, Heinzl & Roithmayr 2007, p. 23; Mertens et al. 2005, pp. 153ff; Turowski 2003, pp. 5f, pp. 99ff). On the other hand, the contents of the research articles can also be understood as planning topics in the sense of creative and goal-oriented leadership with information engineering relation, and then they can be classified as *information management* within business informatics (Ferstl & Sinz 2008, pp. 433f; Hansen & Neumann 2009, p. 240; Heinrich & Lehner 2005, pp. 7f).

The business management-oriented perception – as well as the general management science – typically structures tasks with regard to their strategical, tactical, or operational ranges of consideration (Ferstl & Sinz 2008, p. 79, pp. 438f; Hansen & Neumann 2009, p. 242; Heinrich & Lehner 2005, pp. 22f; Heinrich, Heinzl & Roithmayr 2007, pp. 216f). This business management-oriented structure determines the structure of the book's main part. Figure I-2 illustrates the organization of the book.

The strategic level of *long-term* frame conditions defines encompassing, comprehensive principles and concepts on a horizon of at least three or four years. For this long-term and rather abstract and general perception, the notion of planning in certain respects is too closely defined yet. A long-term strategy formulates convenient policies, guidelines, norms, and standards that yield mission-critical advantages for the basic configuration of the required development schemes and plans. One important point of the strategic arrangements is to preset defaults for downstream tactical issues, for example, related to the assignment of priorities when several stakeholders pursue different or conflicting interests.

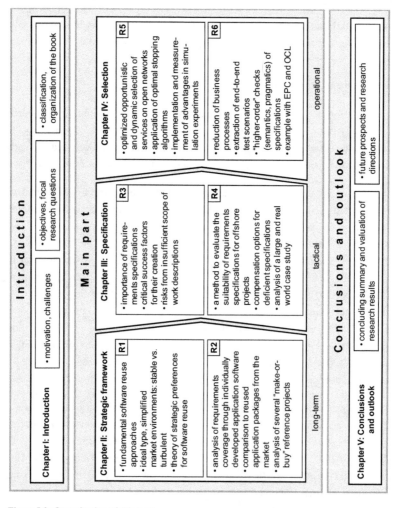

Figure I-2: Organization of this book.

The *tactical* aspects (for which also other names are in use, such as administrative aspects) concern the short and medium-term realization of strategic targets. Tactical aspects can be subsumed, for instance, in a business, program or project planning. Strategic presets and defaults are broken down into a structured set of single targets and tasks, and are put to work to consequently fulfill the strategy. The main topic is the planning and control of the actual process execution including, among other things, resource management, communication, reporting, and escalation procedures.

Finally, *operational* methods and techniques concretely endorse the performing of single development tasks in day to day business operations where details depend on the situation. Tactical parameters help to frame the operational scope of actions and establish a corridor of options that provides clearance and flexibility for operational decisions.

Developing application software systems is a complex activity that cannot be mastered in one sweep. Instead, the development is structured into a systematic process with consecutive individual steps. The overall structure of such development processes is outlined in so-called process models, which can be described as certain phase schemes that provide a structure for the whole development action. By now, several process models have been discussed in theory and used in practice. Synopses of established process models can, for example, be found in the textbooks from Hansen and Neumann (2009, pp. 364-383) or Sametinger (1997, pp. 151-158), specifically for component- and service-oriented development, for example, in Turowski (2003, pp. 112ff). Not least driven from the success of distributed open source development projects – such as the Linux operating system or the Open Office application package – established process models have been scrutinized and broadened as to their implicit basic assumptions since Raymond (1998) at the latest. An important extension to established process models towards component- and service-oriented construction principles has been proposed with the multi-path process model (Ortner 1998, p. 332; Overhage 2006, p. 136). The multi-path process model can be seen as a meta process model, it appears as an extension and unification of existing process models aiming at strategic software reuse. In that, the strategic framework from main part II of this book can be situated within the multi-path model.

Process models are phase schemes that purport frame conditions for tactical planning and decision making. In general and coarsely simplified, software development process models proceed from *Lasten* (requirements) via *Pflichten* (architecture, design) towards implementation and (acceptance-)testing. The individual steps of the process models can be (and usually are) iterative, distributed, and supported by accompanying measures, such as quality assurance or project management. In one way or the other, the specification of requirements is a central constituent in all important development process models. In fact, requirements specification is accepted to be an exceedingly critical step in the software development cycle (Alpar et al. 2008, p. 294; Sommerville 2001, p. 107). Requirements specifications can even be seen as the single most basic and inevitable foundation for each kind of a construction process, cf., for instance, Pahl et al. (2003, pp. 9f). The importance of requirements specifications increases even more in component- and service-oriented application software development approaches. These approaches propagate black box style software reuse where dependencies between the reused elements are explicitly specified (Garlan, Allen & Ockerbloom 1995, p. 25). High quality requirements specifications are gaining further importance also from the increasing trend towards globally divided software development work with offshore parts in downstream development steps of design and implementation phases. From the plethora of tactical issues in the (reuse-driven) development of component- and service-oriented application software systems, the tactical main part III of this book, therefore, is concerned with specification.

Taking the customers' demand viewpoint in the component-based mission statement from Turowski (2003, pp. 9-15), the intention is to procure already existing, external components and services and reuse them in their own context. The identification and selection of appropriate reusable components and services is one of the major challenges then. Therefore, two different methods for the improvement of component and service selection are proposed in the operational main part IV of this book.

Within the business informatics discipline, this book is in line with the mission statement of component- and service-oriented development of application software systems (Turowski 2003, pp. 9-15) and with the process elements of respective construction methodologies (Overhage & Turowski 2008, pp. 112f). Strategic software reuse, hand in hand with component- and service-oriented construction principles, is the starting point and background theme of this book.

The research articles in the main part of this book are further organized according to the business management-oriented distinction between strategical, tactical, and operational ranges of sight. The long-term strategic framework of the main part follows the multi-path process model of component- and service-oriented development. The tactically focused research articles of the main part deal with specification as the central and critical part of the development. The operationally focused research articles of the main part propose methods for the improved selection of components and services from the demand viewpoint.

References

Alpar, P.; Grob, H.; Weimann, P.; Winter, R. (2008), *Anwendungsorientierte Wirtschaftsinformatik: Strategische Planung, Entwicklung und Nutzung von Informations- und Kommunikationssystemen*, 5th edn, Vieweg, Wiesbaden.

Atkinson, C.; Bunse, C.; Groß, H.; Kühne, T. (2002), "Towards a general component model for Web-based applications", *Annals of Software Engineering*, 13 (1): 35-69.

Biggerstaff, T.; Richter, C. (1987), "Reusability framework, assessment, and directions", *IEEE Software*, 4 (2): 41-49.

Boehm, B. (1986), *Wirtschaftliche Software-Produktion*, Forkel, Wiesbaden.

Brandon, D. (2006), *Project management for modern information systems*, IRM Press, Hershey, USA.

Brooks, F. (1987), "No silver bullet: Essence and accidents of software engineering", *IEEE Computer*, 20 (4): 10-19.

Brown, A. (2000), *Large-scale, component-based development*, Prentice Hall, Upper Saddle River, USA.

Chatzoglou, P. (1997), "Factors affecting completion of the requirements capture stage of projects with different characteristics", *Information and Software Technology*, 39 (9): 627-640.

DeMarco, T. (1997), *Warum ist Software so teuer? Und andere Rätsel des Informationszeitalters*, Hanser, Munich.

Dahl, O.; Nygaard, K. (1966), "SIMULA – an ALGOL-based simulation language", *Communications of the ACM*, 9 (9): 671-678.

Dijkstra, E. (1972), "The humble programmer", *Communications of the ACM*, 15 (10): 859-866.

Ferstl, O.; Sinz, E. (2008), *Grundlagen der Wirtschaftsinformatik*, 6th edn, Oldenbourg, Munich.

Fröschle, H.; Reinheimer, S. (eds) (2007), "Serviceorientierte Architekturen", *HMD – Praxis der Wirtschaftsinformatik*, 43 (253).

Garlan, D.; Allen, R.; Ockerbloom, J. (1995), "Architectural mismatch: Why reuse is so hard", *IEEE Software*, 12 (6): 17-26.

Glass, R. (1996), "Study supports existence of software crisis: Management issues appear to be prime cause", *Journal of Systems and Software*, 32 (3): 183-184.

Glass, R. (2005), "'Silver bullet' milestones in software history", *Communications of the ACM*, 48 (8): 15-18.

Glass, R. (2006), "Looking into the challenges of complex IT projects", *Communications of the ACM*, 49 (11): 15-17.

Hansen, H.; Neumann, G. (2009), *Wirtschaftsinformatik 1: Grundlagen und Anwendung*, 10th edn, Lucius & Lucius, Stuttgart.

Heinrich, L.; Heinzl, A.; Roithmayr, F. (2007), *Wirtschaftsinformatik: Einführung und Grundlegung*, 3rd edn, Oldenbourg, Munich.

Heinrich, L.; Lehner, F. (2005), *Informationsmanagement*, 8th edn, Oldenbourg, Munich.

Henderson, J.; Venkatraman, N. (1993), "Strategic alignment: Leveraging information technology for transforming organizations", *IBM Systems Journal*, 32 (1): 4-16.

Martin, R.; Chang, C. (1994), "How to solve the management crisis", *IEEE Software*, 11 (6): 14-15.

Mertens, P.; Bodendorf, F.; König, W.; Picot, A.; Schumann, M.; Hess, T. (2005), *Grundzüge der Wirtschaftsinformatik*, 9th edn, Springer, Berlin.

Meyer, B. (1990), *Objektorientierte Softwareentwicklung*, Hanser, Munich.

Mili, H.; Mili, F.; Mili, A. (1995), "Reusing software: Issues and research directions", *IEEE Transactions on Software Engineering*, 21 (6): 528-562.

Moore, G. (1965), "Cramming more components onto integrated circuits", *Electronics Magazine*, 38 (8): 114-117.

Naur, P.; Randell, B. (Hrsg.) (1969), *Software engineering: Report on a conference sponsored by the NATO Science Committee*, NATO Scientific Affairs Division, Brussels, Belgium.

Neighbors, J. (1984), "The draco approach to constructing software from reusable components", *IEEE Transactions on Software Engineering*, 10 (5):564-574.

Ortner, E. (1998), "Ein Multipfad-Vorgehensmodell für die Entwicklung von Informationssystemen – dargestellt am Beispiel von Workflow-Management Anwendungen", *Wirtschaftsinformatik*, 40 (4): 329-337.

Overhage, S. (2006), "Vereinheitlichte Spezifikation von Komponenten: Grundlagen, UnSCom Spezifikationsrahmen und Anwendung", Dissertation, Universität Augsburg, Augsburg.

Overhage, S.; Turowski, K. (2008), "Ingenieurmäßige Entwicklung von Komponenten, Services und Anwendungssystemen: Zum Aufbau einer Konstruktionslehre für die (Wirtschafts-)Informatik", in Heinemann, E. (ed.), *Anwendungsinformatik: Die Zukunft des Enterprise Engineering*, Nomos, Baden-Baden: 105-119.

Pahl, G.; Beitz, W.; Feldhusen, J.; Grote, K. (2003), *Konstruktionslehre: Grundlagen erfolgreicher Produktentwicklung: Methoden und Anwendung*, 5th edn, Springer, Berlin.

Parnas, D. (1985), "Software aspects of strategic defense systems", *Communications of the ACM*, (28) 12: 1326-1335.

Potok, T.; Vouk, M.; Rindos, A. (1999), "Productivity analysis of object-oriented software developed in a commercial environment", *Software Practice and Experience*, 29 (10): 833-847.

Poulin, J. (1997), *Measuring software reuse: Principles, practices, and economic models*, Addison Wesley, Reading, USA.

Raymond, E. (1998), "The cathedral and the bazaar", *First Monday*, 3 (3).

Rosenau, M. (1981), *Successful project management: A step-by-step approach with practical examples*, Van Nostrand Reinhold, New York, USA.

Rost, J. (1997), "Wiederverwendbare Software", *Wirtschaftsinformatik*, 39 (4): 357-365.

Rumbaugh, J.; Blaha, M.; Premerlami, W.; Eddy, F.; Lorensen, W. (1993), *Objektorientiertes Modellieren und Entwerfen*, Hanser, Munich.

Sackman, H.; Erikson, W.; Grant, E. (1968), "Exploratory experimental studies comparing online and offline programming performance", *Communications of the ACM*, (11) 1: 3-11.

Sametinger, J. (1997), *Software engineering with reusable components*, Springer, Berlin.

Schulte, R. (1996), "'Service oriented' architectures, part 2", Gartner Research ID Number SPA-401-069, Gartner, Stamford, USA.

Schulte, R.; Natis, Y. (1996), "'Service oriented' architectures, part 1", Gartner Research ID Number SPA-401-068, Gartner, Stamford, USA.

Sommerville, I. (2001), *Software engineering*, 6th edn, Pearson, Munich.

Szyperski, C. (1998), *Component software: Beyond object-oriented programming*, Addison Wesley, Harlow, UK.

Teubner, A. (2006), "IT / business alignment", *Wirtschaftsinformatik*, 48 (5): 368-371.

Turowski, K. (2003), *Fachkomponenten: Komponentenbasierte betriebliche Anwendungssysteme*, Shaker, Aachen.

Voas, J. (2001), "Faster, better, and cheaper", *IEEE Software*, 18 (3): 96-97.

Wassermann, A.; Gutz, S. (1982), "The future of programming", *Communications of the ACM*, 25 (3): 196-206.

Wikipedia (2009), "Observable universe", accessed on 17 Jul. 2009, http://en.wikipedia.org/wiki/Observable_ universe.

Wissenschaftliche Kommission Wirtschaftsinformatik (1994), "Profil der Wirtschaftsinformatik", *Wirtschaftsinformatik*, 36 (1): 80-81.

Wissenschaftliche Kommission Wirtschaftsinformatik (2003), *Rahmenempfehlung für die Universitätsausbildung in Wirtschaftsinformatik*, Gesellschaft für Informatik, Bonn.

II Strategic framework

II.R1 A theory of software reuse strategies in ideal type stable and turbulent market environments [1]

Increasingly, information systems need to better support objectives on the overall business strategy level. Software reuse is a promising concept discussed in development organizations in this context, since it is one key issue in designing and delivering information systems and software applications. Reuse is a higher-level strategy with its scope reaching from beyond project boundaries to global markets. Consequently, market conditions can be considered in software reuse management strategies.

With the emergence of modern, turbulent "high-tech" market environments that co-exist with traditional, more stable business conditions of the "old economy", the following research article investigates these two different, ideal type market environments, their business strategies, and related compositional and generative software reuse options. It investigates supporting experience from three large projects, builds theory, and concludes with two hypotheses on strategic management preferences for software reuse.

Supporting the analysis, the experiences from three large practical projects are presented. Consequently, a respective long-term reuse theory is founded and formulated in two hypotheses on strategic management preferences for software reuse. According to that theory, generative reuse is preferred rather in traditional stable markets while compositional reuse is beneficial rather under turbulent market conditions.

---

[1] Research article R1: Skroch, O.; Turowski, K. (2009), "A theory of software reuse strategies in ideal type stable and turbulent market environments", *Proceedings of the 15th Americas Conference on Information Systems*, Association for Information Systems, 6-9 Aug. 2009, San Francisco, USA: 272.

1   Introduction and objectives

The paramount relevance of IS (information systems) for today's businesses is being studied since many years, and strategies to leverage aligned business value (Henderson & Venkatraman 1993; Luftman, Papp & Brier 1999) from IS assets have become vital in many markets. For software businesses it was even mentioned that "value creation is the final arbiter of success […] In particular, there is a deeper understanding of the role of strategy in creating value" (Boehm & Sullivan 2000).

Software reuse is an important and promising strategic approach pursued for applications and IS to stipulate, contribute and align to business values. Reuse was recognized as a financial investment (Barnes & Bollinger 1991) and the relative costs of building IS from reuse, as opposed to building them for reuse, have been studied (Favaro 1991). As mentioned by Favaro (1996), value based principles for the management of reuse in the enterprise advocate the maximization of economic value as governing objective. The idea that "business decisions drive reuse" (Poulin 1997) was pointed out. Management processes of reuse were investigated, including the idea that reuse concepts evolve with increased investment and experience (Jacobson, Griss & Jonsson 1997). Strategic planning and metrics of reuse in large corporations were discussed in detail (Lim 1998).

While reuse offers various options and advantages today, one of the major remaining challenges is "a deeper understanding of when to use particular methods, based, for example, on […] business context" (Frakes & Kang 2005). This paper proposes a theory on this subject. It investigates strategic reuse options in software businesses and their potential value propositions in the context of two model type market environments with their core strategies.

Strategic management options in software processes can be explained in the multi-path process model in Figure II.R1-1, based on Ortner (1998) and Overhage (2006). The model proposes four strategy levels – individual solution, component solution, off-the-shelf solution and outsourcing. Two levels emphasize overall IS and applications: off-the-shelf solution implies the introduction of COTS (commercial off-the-shelf) applications, and outsourcing aims at service level agreements with 3rd party suppliers. Focus of this theory is on the two deeper multi-path levels which relate to organizations centered on software development aspects: individual solution and component solution. We recognize that these two levels imply different focal points for reuse, and we apply a classic distinction introduced by Biggerstaff and Richter (1987) associating *generative reuse* and *compositional reuse* with the two levels.

With highly specific features of an individual solution, focus is on the design and implementation of the new features *for* reuse, e.g. in other projects or on global markets. With common features of a component solution, focus is on IS design *from* reusable components, e.g. from catalogues or, again, global markets. These two reuse options differ widely in terms of management, applicability, and value contribution.

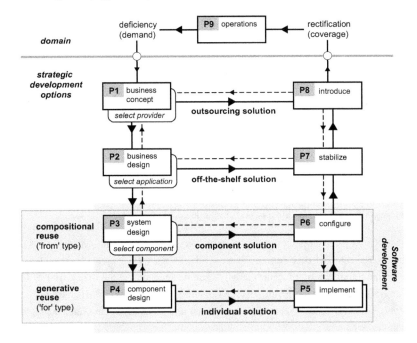

Figure II.R1-1: Strategic options in the multi-path process model.

On the business strategy level, management needs (among other things) strong market-orientation for sustaining success. Market conditions purport business objectives; therefore we examine two different, ideal type business conditions and their respective market player strategies: *defenders* in traditional stable markets of diminishing returns and *prospectors* in turbulent "high-tech" markets of increasing returns. We show that underlying competition styles differ, drive distinct business goals and stipulate different entrepreneurial, managerial, engineering and administrative decisions (Miles & Snow 1978; Arthur 1996). Therefore, different value propositions are required, including specifically also software reuse approaches.

Combining these considerations, we derive a theory of reuse options supporting business strategies under the two market conditions. Similar theory building approaches have recently been taken e.g. to align IS architecture to business interaction patterns (Schlueter-Langdon 2003), to manage IT-enabled decision support in turbulent environments (Carlsson & El Sawy 2008), or to examine the contribution of network-based market environments to the domain of information and communication technology (Rossignoli 2009).

Development of reasonable theory is a central activity in research and is traditionally based on a combination of previous theory and literature, common sense and experience, e.g. (Eisenhardt 1989; Yin 2003). Theory building, as research in its own right, precedes empirical hypothesis testing. Accordingly, this paper takes first steps first and constructs theory from the analysis of previously existing theories and literature, and from well-understood cases from practical experience.

2   Basic software reuse options

Many definitions exist for the concept of software reuse. We give two examples only – "the degree to which a software module or other work product can be used in more than one computer program or software system" (IEEE Standards Board 1990) and "the process of creating systems from existing software rather than building systems from scratch" (Krueger 1992) – and state that most reuse definitions implicitly suggest the intention to capitalize on pre-existing assets and knowledge already acquired in the past.

A widely accepted taxonomy proposed already by Biggerstaff and Richter (1987) distinguishes compositional reuse from generative reuse. This is so elementary that it can repeatedly be found under other names, e.g. "reuse techniques" (Prieto-Díaz 1993), or "software reuse technical tools" (Lim 1998). Table II.R1-1 is based on Biggerstaff and Richter (1987), provides an overview of compositional and generative reuse, and mentions some of their characteristics.

Reuse Strategy	Compositional	Generative
Reused Entity	building blocks	solution patterns
Nature of Entity	atomic and immutable, passive	diffuse and malleable, active
Emphasis	repositories (markets), composition principles	generators, processes
Examples	class library, Web service, component	4th generation language, code generator, design pattern

Table II.R1-1: Fundamental reuse strategies.

The compositional idea aims at directly reusing binary artifacts from repositories or markets to put together large applications. The generative method "is based on the reuse of a generation process" (Sametinger 1997) which is a higher level of abstraction and works indirectly by generating, partly automated, software from abstract patterns or models.

Business value creation from software reuse depends upon its field of adoption and the higher ranking business objectives derived (among others) from market environments. Reuse can for example reduce the time required to create or modify enterprise applications, providing increased adaptation capabilities and shortened delivery timescales for the enterprise (Lim 1998). Or, combining individually programmed applications with COTS systems can lead to optimized application portfolios, delivering higher quality with reduced lifecycle costs to the enterprise (Orfali, Harkey & Edwards 1996). Therefore strategic management decisions on reuse can make a difference and require consideration.

2.1 Compositional reuse – building blocks

In compositional reuse, prefabricated artifacts are reused to assemble large applications. The vision is, eventually, to establish a software components industry. This concept can be traced back to the 1960s (McIlroy 1969). Compositional reuse can be understood from the idea of *modularity* in systems theory (Simon 1981) and software engineering (Parnas 1972) among others. By assembling modular compounds from smaller sub-compounds that can be designed independently yet function together as a whole, traditional industries (e.g. electronics, automotive) have experienced previously unknown levels of innovation and growth, e.g. Baldwin and Clark (1999). Software businesses set out to follow such success stories through reusable binary software components (Szyperski, Gruntz & Murer 2002). But building IS from compositional reuse remains difficult. While component trading has arrived on (electronic) markets – e.g. for Web services, which can be seen as flavors of compositional reuse (Atkinson et al. 2002) – it has not become mainstream practice yet. Among the reason mentioned is the insufficient maturity of the software engineering discipline with its particular absence of commonly accepted standards (Hahn & Turowski 2005).

An important managerial issue in compositional reuse is the black box type of access the reusing party has to the component. Black box reuse employs existing assets in plug and play style without modification, only on the basis of a specified behavior at the interfaces, e.g. Brown (2000). Black box style reuse inevitably is restrained by the design that was chosen for the implementation of the selected components. This design cannot be changed and if a certain component behaves differently from specific design constraints in the overall IS then its reuse adds no value, because it might be inefficient or even impossible to fit in this particular component.

2.2 Generative reuse – solution patterns

Leading generative reuse approaches include scavenging, generative programming, model-driven architecture and product-line engineering. In scavenging (Krueger 1992), fragments of source code are copied. Generative programming (Czarnecki & Eisenecker 2000) automatically creates software through configuration within a predefined solution space. Model-driven architecture (Soley 2000) captures core software assets as platform-independent models and automatically derives the implementations. Product-line engineering (Weiss & Lai 1999) groups IS development around families of products and manages commonalities and variabilities.

Generative reuse works on a higher abstraction level as compared to compositional reuse, and in particular it is independent from implementation. It can be explained from the fundamental idea of *pattern abstractions*. Alexander et al. (1977) first presented the pattern approach and defined "pattern languages" as sets of abstract, well-proven solutions for reoccurring problems which emerge as the related domain develops. The pattern idea was also embraced in software businesses for reusing suitable solutions and concepts that have been worked out and used successfully before. Patterns became widely accepted with object-oriented design patterns (Gamma et al. 1995) latest. Pattern abstractions have been identified, described and used for many more aspects since then.

Significant managerial issues with generative reuse are its domain specific quality and the operational difficulties with generators that synthesize software for a target IS. Patterns are specific for a business, industry, market or domain. They alone lack the implementation paragraph required for reuse. The generative reuse approach is therefore based on the reuse of both a (formalized) pattern abstraction and a generative process (automatically) creating the reused entity from this abstraction.

3   Two ideal type market environments and their business strategy

Two different model types of market environments can be distinguished as shown in Table II.R1-2: traditional stable markets of diminishing returns and turbulent markets of increasing returns (Arthur 1996). The traditional view on markets as coordination mechanisms describes development on substitutable resources. Players expand in perfect competition until eventually a stable equilibrium is established that generates small predictable margins with prices at the average production cost. But observations in modern "high-tech" businesses reveal a different scenario with markets that develop on knowledge with the first winning mover out of a turbulent uncertainty being able to lock the market into an instable positive feedback loop thus generating large margins. Following Miles and Snow (1978), typical players in these two environments can be characterized as defenders and prospectors.

While real market conditions will rarely reflect one of these two ideal sides in full clarity, we start with a "reductionist" view and acknowledge that both market environments represent two aspects of reality that fundamentally differ in their underlying economics, their character of competition, their entrepreneurial, managerial, engineering and administrative problems, and their related business strategies. They present different challenges for software management, and consequently for the issue of reuse strategies, too.

Market Environment	Traditional	Turbulent
Dynamics	quite stable	highly dynamic
Returns	diminishing	increasing
Processing	resources	information
Business Models	mature, well established	changing, unprecedented
Competitive Drivers	risk avoidance, cost control, quality assurance	innovation, time to market, flexibility
Typical Player	defender with internal focus	prospector with external focus
Strategy	constant internal improvement at low risk	rapid adaptation to external changes

Table II.R1-2: Two ideal type market environments.

3.1 Traditional environments – defenders

Traditional markets reflect the 19th century Marshall view of economic machinery that processes substitutable resources. Characteristics of such markets are established and steady market shares in supply, together with noticeable preferences in demand. Most suppliers share a common level of highly developed technologies, products and services. Collaboration is well established, markets "act" as coordination mechanisms and prices reach equilibrium at the average cost of production, which is stable since it generates small predictable margins. Often there are accepted quality standards, sometimes even legally enforced, and de facto pricing categories for products and services exist.

Agents that get ahead eventually face limitations from rising costs (e.g. resource shortage) or falling profits (e.g. increased competition). This can be explained from the high maturity levels that such businesses have passed through. Challenges from unforeseen innovations are unlikely and no strategic management issue, since no player is actually able to corner the market. Stable market environments are associated with the "old economy" of diminishing returns. A typical player in this environment is the defender organization that devotes primary attention to improving the efficiency of its existing operations (Miles & Snow 1978).

3.1.1 Defensive internal improvement strategies

In businesses characterized by defensive internal improvement strategies, competitors can hardly dislodge established players from their positions, and only major market shifts would create actual opportunities or threats. Management perspectives therefore remain centered on efficient and well-proven technologies. Defenders are managed towards maintaining stability and efficiency, while they are not prepared to face changes. Consequently, larger investments are reasonable only for technological problems that remain common and unsurprising for a longer period (Miles & Snow 1978).

Business strategy is towards avoiding risks and permanently reducing costs at high and stable quality levels. Management steadily improves the repeating processes and sustains slow but continuous long-term improvement in small steps. This can be achieved by constant internal optimization and quality assurance, by planning and hierarchical control (Arthur 1996).

Under stable market conditions, IS advance continuously, too. A process of successive maturation has finally resulted in grown and mature legacy applications and a well practiced business process routine. Both are well aligned and efficiently support a stable business. IS and software applications are regarded as a *commodity*, and the associated IT processes have become routine tasks, too. But there is small and steady market pressure to always slightly improve competitiveness. Further enhancements on top of the already achieved levels are therefore very sophisticated features above the established standards.

Management generally prefers reuse to building software from scratch in such environments. Generative reuse in particular provides more control and promises lower life cycle costs through automation and generators. Patterns for reuse can be discovered (only) in stable and repeating processes. The more a certain domain evolves, the more patterns can be discovered. Documented patterns represent domain specific, highly specialized improvement potential to still deliver lower costs while not decreasing quality. In generative approaches, patterns and models are explicitly documented and therefore can be tailored during the generative process, too. The generative process also implicitly improves measurement and control of the generated software quality.

The time and complexity of realizing generative reuse in particular includes the laborious and difficult formalization of the underlying models and the building of software generators. This can be acceptable in this environment, as long as higher optimization levels are reached while competition remains stable, and a positive long-time return is assured.

3.1.2   Defenders' dilemma

Managing such defensive strategy faces an important dilemma: with increasing sophistication of businesses, IS, and application software, further improvement is attended by higher efforts while at the same time marginal gains decline. Another incremental improvement might always be found, but the increments become smaller, the related efforts grow, and beyond a certain point negative returns might result – even with formal models and automation.

Compositional reuse seems no option here since it would assume, as a prerequisite, the availability of suitable components that provide factual advantages. While it is very likely that high quality prefabricated components exist in mature markets, it is unlikely that these will provide any competitive edge. Their functionalities and qualities will be close to established de facto standards and therefore they will neither threat (respectively help) an established player, nor will they provide true, unique advantages to newcomers.

In brief, the analysis of traditional business environments with defensive market players suggests the theory that management follows low risk optimization strategies and considers especially the generative reuse option.

3.2 Turbulent environments – prospectors

Turbulent markets are described from the outstanding performance of the "high-tech" sector in the late 1990s (Gordon 2000). Such environments are characterized as ICT (information and communication technology) driven (Klodt 2001). These markets are only loosely regulated, highly complex and unstable, and face coordination challenges. New goods based on intangible resources are created rapidly. They alter quickly and unpredictably, and change during IS development. Market entry barriers are high: new technologies require significant up-front engagement with the risk of an uncertain outcome.

These markets always change and players and collaborations rapidly emerge and vanish. But successful players can grow at high rates and realize excessive margins, since the markets show "winner-takes-all" properties: the first successful mover is able to lock a market for the own product or service. Turbulent markets spread, because of the increasing importance of intangible resources (information, knowledge, etc.), which in parallel becomes widely and cheaply available (through software, on the Internet, etc.) (Boehm 2005). Most of their dynamics can be explained in traditional terms and no new strategic textbooks are required (Porter 2001).

We associate turbulent markets with increasing returns environments (Katz & Shapiro 1985; Elsner 2004). A typical player characteristic for this environment is the prospector organization that embraces change and shows a strong concern for product and market innovation (Miles & Snow 1978).

3.2.1 Prospective rapid adaptation strategies

In businesses characterized by prospective external adaptation strategies, players meet changing conditions with own innovations, but run the risk of overextending their resources. Management focus is on technological flexibility to enable rapid responses, while maximum efficiency cannot develop. Prospectors are managed to maintain flexibility but may not optimally utilize their resources (Miles & Snow 1978).

Business strategy is towards rapid external adaptation, as unpredictable situations demand reactivity and quick response from management. Prospectors are managed as mission-oriented organizations which compete for the next winning business model or technology, and the winner will take most. Hence it is imperative to enter the market first if possible, with a new business model and IS that work *well enough* to support the new business and become widely accepted (Arthur 1996).

The associated IS are completely new or even not existing yet. Moreover, in turbulent "high-tech" environments the IS are often expected to stipulate new business models or support new business functions for the first time in the market. Such ideas permanently appear and vanish and management has little indication of their longer term significance.

To still support the overall business strategy, the organization needs to be primarily managed towards high flexibility. Flexibility in building IS originates in low development efforts. Compositional reuse reduces efforts and provides flexibility by assembling IS from ready-to-use components that are loosely "plugged" onto frameworks. Management can minimize overall efforts through skillful demarcation of the domain and through covering demanded features with existing components where possible. Related IS might then start as component tapestry, put together ad hoc to satisfy the current business well enough. In unstable domain parts, the IS adopts by exchanging components. In parts that become stable the IS evolve into persistent domain specific frameworks.

3.2.2   Prospectors' dilemma

Management encounters the main dilemma for prospectors: the IS life cycle is unknown beforehand. Many ideas for new products and services are brought forward but their commercial prospects can hardly be predicted. Organizations need to be prepared to start over from zero again and again, chasing new ideas as they appear. At the same time, if a business, product or service survives, supporting IS that were quickly plugged together might have to be sustained, possibly over a longer period of time, until they are eventually either replaced or become properly institutionalized.

Generative reuse seems no option here since there is little maturity in these continuously changing environments and few if any patterns can be identified. A situation will rarely reappear, and the successful reuse of patterns is unlikely. Also the amount of time and effort required to prepare and maintain formal models and generators opposes the business strategy.

In brief, the analysis of turbulent business environments with prospective market players suggests the theory that management follows fast external adaptation strategies and favors especially the compositional reuse option.

4   Supporting experience: projects from practice

We support our assumptions through three selected projects which we were involved in between 2000 and 2005 (the reports had to be made anonymous, which does not affect their arguments). The experience provides valid substantiation for our suggestions. This is not meant as empirical evidence to test our theory, which is a subsequent step after having derived reasonable hypotheses in the first place. But it is a core element in theory building, as described e.g. by Eisenhardt (1989).

4.1   Stable environment – fraud detection

A multinational corporation was working in a holding-type structure with one head quarter and several operative units on two continents. The head quarter received management reports from all units in a central reporting database. This procedure was highly standardized, most steps were automated. Certain reappearing irregularities in the figures were found manually and management suspected a new type of fraud. A self-learning fraud detection tool was used as part of the IS since long on all reporting figures as part of the daily processes. This tool was made individually for the firm, but it failed to identify the new fraud type.

No functionality recognizing this specific irregularity was available as prefabricated solution. No market demand for such highly specific feature existed, hence no supply either. The feature was then implemented individually to enhance the existing IS, which could deal with a whole new fraud class afterwards. The implementation also used existing software automation tools for generating code skeletons.

In this stable environment, generative reuse worked well on a bespoke functionality, its pattern abstraction, and the partly automated generation of software from that abstraction. Compositional reuse would have failed because no component existed for the highly specific requirement.

4.2   Turbulent environment – software simulator

One of the leading diversified corporations world-wide acquired a base technology patent and created a business case for it. The new technology had to be simulated by software first, to prove that the technology works in principle and to clear the budget for a physical prototype.

A number of simulation software product suites were available on the market. The actual simulation requirements were not fully understood and it was expected that they would change during development. Coding from scratch was recognized as inevitable for most parts of the simulation core. But for the general parts of the simulator, e.g. user interfaces, random number generation, scenario logging and replay, etc., standard components could be found and put together. Meanwhile, all specific new functionality was developed from scratch.

In this "high-tech" business situation, compositional reuse worked well to quickly deliver unspecific functions, while coding from scratch was minimized to the new features. Generative reuse would have failed because it is impossible to identify patterns and implement a generative process for a solution that is unknown at development time.

4.3   Hybrid environment – portal architecture

A large multinational publisher ran its print products business very successfully since decades. Business was managed decentrally, and each subsidiary had own IS landscapes consisting of COTS and a number of individually created tools. The situation was stable and the IS worked nicely in the absence of larger changes.

Following the shift in publishing markets towards digital content, new IS became necessary. Prefabricated portal components available on the market were planned to encapsulate the back-office legacy. Small individually designed back-office amendments, mainly in the form of adaptors, were to enable inter-operability. The implementation approach was to realize the changes in one reference environment, and to reuse this as blueprint in the other subsidiaries.

Market changes shaped a complicated hybrid situation with the traditional business still running while an uncertain new business had to be realized. The target IS was based on compositional reuse to provide new functionality for the new business lines, and generative reuse to encapsulate legacy applications supporting the traditional businesses.

5   Concluding hypotheses, limitations and further steps

We investigated software reuse strategies and saw that there are two fundamental options for organizations building software applications for large IS: compositional reuse based on assembling prefabricated components, and generative reuse based on models, patterns and generators. We also investigated two ideal type business conditions, stable and turbulent, each with typical players, defenders and prospectors, with their typical business strategies.

Combining the concepts, we argued that generative reuse is more likely to yield value for defenders in traditional stable environments where marginal gains are low and improvements difficult to achieve. In contrast, we argued that compositional reuse is more likely to be useful for prospectors in turbulent businesses because it is faster. We strengthened our argument with experience from three selected projects, not as a test of theory but as one step in building reasonable theory in the first place. Essentially, we believe that successful software reuse management delivers low risk improvements for defensive business strategies rather through generative reuse concepts, and short time-to-market for prospective business strategies rather through compositional reuse approaches.

We can state this as two hypotheses now:

- Generative reuse is an adequate strategic software reuse management option in traditional stable markets characterized by defender organizations.

- Compositional reuse is an adequate strategic software reuse management option in turbulent dynamic markets characterized by prospector organizations.

Table II.R1-3 briefly sums up the synthesis of the hypotheses. Managerial implications include the need to assess the type of market environment for the considered business, product, or service, with their supporting IS. With the type of market environment as one influence factor, management could then derive an unspecific preference for a software reuse strategy option.

Market Player	Defender	Prospector
Market environment	traditional	turbulent
Strategic focus	constant internal improvement at low risk	rapid adaptation to external opportunities and threats
IS and software applications	grown legacy systems, highly evolved	ad hoc / none, frameworks
Reuse objectives	well-understood and proven patterns, improvement in small increments	low development efforts, being fast and "good enough"
Dilemma	declining cost-benefit ratio	unknown system life cycles
Preferred reuse strategy	generative	compositional

Table II.R1-3: Reuse options and market players.

Our theory is limited by the fact that real situations show highly complex, multifaceted markets, businesses, IS, and software applications, with a growing importance of increasing returns effects (Boehm 2005; Samavi, Yu & Topaloglou 2009). The model type market environments – which we deliberately had to assume to find a "reductionist" starting point for theory development – are only weak approximations of real market conditions. Moreover, there are other important factors influencing strategic software reuse decisions apart from market environments, which is also out of scope of the present theory. Further limitations come from the fact that real life management alternatives are seldom fully confined model type options, and e.g. Llorens et al. (2006) reason about advantages of a holistic "incremental software reuse" theory (without framing it concretely). Furthermore, as we saw in the hybrid environment case, traditional lines of business can (and often do) exist together with turbulent businesses in one company. Management could e.g. separate out the domains, but our present strategic hypotheses do not focus on related operational issues. The hypotheses are no broad software reuse strategy guide, but a step towards recognizing adequate strategic reuse preferences that suggest themselves in opposing market environments. Finally, our theory is only constructed by now and not empirically confirmed yet. Main contribution of this work is that we could constitute – by reasonably reducing considerations – two concrete hypotheses of software reuse management strategies in different market environments. This qualitative theory building approach can now be expanded by a quantitative approach to challenge the theory and to establish reconfirmed ex-ante management strategy support as also ex-post assessment frameworks that can help to approximate the diligence of software management strategies.

References

Alexander, C.; Ishikawa, S.; Silverstein, M.; Jacobson, M.; Fiksdahl-King, I.; Angel, S. (1977), *A pattern language: Towns, buildings, construction*, Oxford University Press, New York, USA.

Arthur, B. (1996), "Increasing returns and the two worlds of business", *Harvard Business Review*, 74 (4): 100-109.

Atkinson, C.; Bunse, C.; Groß H.; Kühne, T. (2002), "Towards a general component model for Web-based applications", *Annals of Software Engineering*, 13 (1): 35-69.

Baldwin, C.; Clark, K. (1999), *Design rules volume 1: The power of modularity*, MIT Press, Cambridge, USA.

Barnes, B.; Bollinger, T. (1991), "Making reuse cost-effective", *IEEE Software*, 8 (1): 13-24.

Biggerstaff, T.; Richter, C. (1987), "Reusability framework, assessment, and directions", *IEEE Software*, 4 (2): 41-49.

Boehm, B. (2005), "The future of software processes", *Unifying the software process spectrum: Proceedings of the international software process workshop: Revised selected papers*, Lecture Notes in Computer Science 3840, Springer, 25-27 May 2005, Beijing, China: 10-24.

Boehm, B.; Sullivan, K. (2000), "Software economics: A roadmap", *Proceedings of the 22nd international conference on software engineering: Future of software engineering track*, ACM, 4-11 Jun. 2000, Limerick, Ireland: 319-343.

Brown, A. (2000), *Large-scale, component-based development*, Prentice Hall, Upper Saddle River, USA.

Carlsson, S.; El Sawy, O. (2008), "Managing the five tensions of IT-enabled decision support in turbulent and high-velocity environments", *Information Systems and e-Business Management*, 6 (3): 225-237.

Czarnecki, K.; Eisenecker, U. (2000), *Generative programming: Methods, tools, and applications*, Addison Wesley, Boston, USA.

Eisenhardt, K. (1989), "Building theories from case study research", *Academy of Management Review*, 14 (4): 532-550.

Elsner, W. (2004), "The 'new' economy: Complexity, coordination and a hybrid governance approach", *International Journal of Social Economics*, 31 (11/12): 1029-1049.

Favaro, J. (1991), "What price reusability? A case study", *ACM SIG Ada – Ada Letters*, 11 (3): 115-124.

Favaro, J. (1996), "Value based principles for management of reuse in the enterprise", *Proceedings of the 4th international conference on software reuse*, IEEE Computer Society, 23-26 Apr. 1996, Orlando, USA: 221-222.

Frakes, W.; Kang, K. (2005), "Software reuse research: Status and future", *IEEE Transactions on Software Engineering*, 31 (7): 529-536.

Gamma, E.; Helm, R.; Johnson, R.; Vlissides, J. (1995), *Design patterns: Elements of reusable object-oriented software*, Addison Wesley, Boston, USA.

Gordon, R. (2000), "Does the 'New Economy' measure up to the great inventions of the past?", *Journal of Economic Perspectives*, 14 (4): 49-74.

Hahn, H.; Turowski, K. (2005), "Modularity of the software industry: A model for the use of standards and alternative coordination mechanisms", *International Journal of IT Standards and Standardization Research*, 3 (2): 68-80.

Henderson, J.; Venkatraman, N. (1993), "Strategic alignment: Leveraging information technology for transforming organizations", *IBM Systems Journal*, 32 (1): 4-16.

IEEE Standards Board (1990), *IEEE standard glossary of software engineering terminology*, IEEE, New York, USA.

Jacobson, I.; Griss, M.; Jonsson, P. (1997), *Software reuse: Architecture, process and organization for business success*, ACM Press, New York, USA.

Katz, M.; Shapiro, C. (1985), "Network externalities, competition, and compatibility", *American Economic Review*, 75 (3): 424-440.

Klodt, H. (2001), "The essence of the new economy", Kiel Discussion Paper 375, Kiel Institute for World Economics, Kiel.

Krueger, C. (1992), "Software reuse", *ACM Computing Surveys*, 24 (2): 131-183.

Lim, W. (1998), *Managing software reuse*, Prentice Hall, Upper Saddle River, USA.

Luftman, J.; Papp, R.; Brier, T. (1999), "Enablers and inhibitors of business-IT alignment", *Communications of the Association for Information Systems*, 1: 11.

Llorens, J.; Fuentes, J.; Prieto-Díaz, R.; Astudillo, H. (2006), "Incremental software reuse", *Reuse of off-the-shelf components: Proceedings of the 9th international conference on software reuse*, Lecture Notes in Computer Science 4039, Springer, 11-14 Jun. 2006, Turin, Italy: 386-389.

McIlroy, M. (1969), "Mass produced software components", *Software engineering: Report on a conference sponsored by the NATO Science Committee*, NATO Scientific Affairs Division, 7-11 Oct. 1968, Garmisch: 138-155.

Miles, R.; Snow, C. (1978), *Organizational strategy, structure, and process*, McGraw Hill, New York, USA.

Orfali, R.; Harkey, D.; Edwards, J. (1996), *The essential distributed objects survival guide*, Wiley, New York, USA.

Ortner, E. (1998), "Ein Multipfad-Vorgehensmodell für die Entwicklung von Informationssystemen – dargestellt am Beispiel von Workflow-Management Anwendungen", *Wirtschaftsinformatik*, 40 (4): 329-337.

Overhage, S. (2006), "Vereinheitlichte Spezifikation von Komponenten: Grundlagen, UnSCom Spezifikationsrahmen und Anwendung", Dissertation, Universität Augsburg, Augsburg.

Parnas, D. (1972), "On the criteria to be used in decomposing systems into modules", *Communications of the ACM*, 15 (12): 1053-1058.

Porter, M. (2001), "Strategy and the Internet", *Harvard Business Review*, 79 (2): 63-78.

Poulin, J. (1997), *Measuring software reuse: Principles, practices, and economic models*, Addison Wesley, Reading, USA.

Prieto-Díaz, R. (1993), "Status report: Software reusability", *IEEE Software*, 10 (3): 61-66.

Rossignoli, C. (2009), "The contribution of transaction cost theory and other network-oriented techniques to digital markets", *Information Systems and e-Business Management*, 7 (1): 57-79.

Samavi, R.; Yu, E.; Topaloglou, T. (2009), "Strategic reasoning about business models: a conceptual modeling approach", *Information Systems and e-Business Management*, 7 (2): 171-198.

Sametinger, J. (1997), *Software engineering with reusable components*, Springer, Berlin.

Schlueter-Langdon, C. (2003), "Information systems architecture styles and business interaction patterns: Toward theoretic correspondence", *Information Systems and e-Business Management*, 1 (3): 283-304.

Simon, H. (1981), *The sciences of the artificial*, MIT Press, Cambridge, USA.

Soley, R. (2000), "Model driven architecture: Object Management Group white paper", OMG, Needham, USA.

Szyperski, C.; Gruntz, D.; Murer, S. (2002), *Component software: Beyond object-oriented programming*, 2nd edn, Addison Wesley, London, UK.

Weiss, D.; Lai, C. (1999), *Software product-line engineering: A family-based software development process*, Addison Wesley, Reading, USA.

Yin, R. (2003), *Case study research: Design and methods*, 3rd edn, Sage, Thousand Oaks, USA.

II.R2 **Integration assessment of an individually developed application vs. software packages from the market – an experience report** [2]

The following research article presents the examination of the results from an IT strategy project performed by a team of consultants from the software engineering sector for a large client in the communications business. The client requirements sketched a highly integrated, inter-organizational business support system. The examination of the project results focus on the "make-or-buy" assessment of individual application software development, as compared to alternative courses of action based on the reuse and integration of software packages and components which are available on the market.

Two main findings are achieved in this paper. First, within twenty functional requirement areas analyzed and compared, advantages could not be found for integrating individually developed software, but for software purchased on the market instead. Second, a selection of seven comparable case studies, despite of being relevant for the client's development and integration scenario, have not conveyed a conclusive picture pro or con individually developed software – suggesting that further critical success factors exist.

---

[2] Research article R2: Skroch, O. (2006), "Integration assessment of an individually developed application vs. software packages from the market – an experience report", *Integration, Informationslogistik und Architektur: Proceedings DW 2006*, Lecture Notes in Informatics P-90, Gesellschaft für Informatik, 21-22 Sep. 2006, Friedrichshafen: 329-340.

1   Introduction and setting

National monopolist providers still dominate fixed wire telecommunications landscapes in many parts of this world. Nevertheless the overall picture started changing since some years, with regulatory bodies promoting privatization and competition, and further players entering the markets put pressure on the incumbents. This has been examined in a survey on the implications of EU (European Union) legislation on telecom providers in the new EU member states (Ewers et al. 2004). Hence, especially communications suppliers that are still monopolists in their markets today have started preparing for a competitive future, e.g. Pyshkin (2003).

One of the core competitive assets in the supply of communications services are information systems. Here, providers typically make the distinction between OSS (operation support systems) and BSS (business support systems). In most definitions, OSS includes all systems that are directly related to the telecom networks themselves and their technical processes, such as network management or IN (intelligent network) platforms. BSS, on the other side, include the downstream applications less directly related to network technology and mainly driven by business needs. Typical examples for BSS functionalities include billing, CRM (customer relationship management), or order processing. The actual mapping of a system or component can be ambiguous and is also subject to change with the NGN (next generation networks) trend or the spread of voice over IP (internet protocol), e.g. Skroch and Turowski (2006). Further topical insight provide for example the ITU-T (International Telecommunication Union – Telecommunication Standardization Sector) Recommendations M Series.

Compared to OSS, the BSS area is much less standardized – even very few accepted industry standards exist. BSS functions are significantly more complex and intertwined, and are expected to be very well aligned to fully integrate the respective providers' businesses. Furthermore, many parts of the BSS in telecoms need to be high-availability and high-performance systems. Finally, many BSS functions are subject to rapid, unexpected and market-driven change, in particular as to the fast implementation of new marketing ideas. BSS suppliers providing respective carrier-grade software systems form a highly fragmented market, e.g. Frost and Sullivan (2003), and many telecom providers, especially the very large ones, still have major parts of their BSS individually developed. Traditional individual software development, however, faces more and more constraints, and related considerations continue in theory as well as in practice (Taubner 2005).

To master this software challenge, next to others the concept of compositional reuse (Biggerstaff & Richter 1987) integrating prefabricated business components traded on markets (Turowski 2003; Szyperski 1998) is pursued in theory and practice since long. It can be seen as complementary alternative to traditional approaches such as individual development today. As early as in 1969 software components were proposed, with catalogues of software parts that can be retrieved and composed to large applications, similar as electronic parts (McIlroy 1969). Later it has even been stated that reuse is the "only realistic approach" to meet the future software needs (Mili, Mili & Mili 1995, p. 528).

Important differences in development and integration approaches, and specifically also peculiarities of procured solutions, component solutions and individual solutions, can be explained in the flexible multi-path process model in Figure II.R2-1. Four development levels are presented in the model. One or more of the levels can be chosen to satisfy an identified requirement through information systems support.

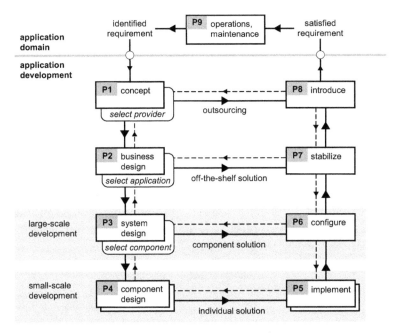

Figure II.R2-1: Multi-path process model. Becker and Overhage (2003, p. 19), based on Ortner (1998, p. 332).

Individual solution for component design means coding programs to implement the features – the so-called "small-scale development"; component solution for system design means that features are covered by composing existing components into a respective configuration – the so-called "large-scale development". Off-the-shelf solution means migrating to standard applications and stabilizing them; outsourcing means defining service level agreements and contracting 3rd party suppliers.

In the experience report presented here, the client wanted to reconsider a strategic IT decision that can be explained as a choice for a development level in the multi-path process model. The client was a very large national telecommunications monopolist, and one of the leading full-service communications providers in the whole region. The client's firm was a multi-company corporation and offered an extensive product and service portfolio including landline and mobile voice communications, data communications including the Internet, complex and custom made corporate solutions, call centers, software development, clearing house services, sea cables and satellite operations, pay TV, smart card manufacturing, etc.

The mission of the client was to replace most parts of the existing home-grown BSS tapestry with a fully integrated corporate wide (i.e. inter-organizational) solution. To realize this, the client started to individually develop respective software from scratch. This process commenced about two years before the reported IT strategy consulting project. The mission had top level management attention at any time, but it still had repeatedly missed its deadlines and had failed to deliver. The corporation finally engaged the consultant to assess the ongoing development, to create an alternative planning based on the integration of software products procured on the market, and finally to compare the running "Make" integration project with "Buy" integration planning expected from the consultant.

2   Project approach and selected results

The client wanted the consultant to support a strategic IT decision regarding the integration of the new BSS solution: continuation of the long running individual development mission that had repeatedly failed to deliver, or switching to the integration of ready-made solutions bought on the market. The client's core drivers for the intended BSS solution were, in order of decreasing relevance: functionality, flexibility, risks, cost, and time to market.

The retrieval and generation of decision relevant information by the consultant was structured in several work areas, among them the following two which can be presented in more detail in this paper:

- Functional comparison of available packages.
- Integration scenario case studies.

The consulting was based on the information provided by the client for the ongoing development and integration project creating a bespoke solution, and on the consultant's expertise in integrating systems made from predefined parts.

2.1   Functional comparison of available packages

The consultant created a comparison between the functionalities provided by five packages available on the market, and the functionalities of the intended individually developed solution. Due to the very broad scope of required functionality, the five market packages chosen by the consultant each consisted of vendor package offers made up from a number of each vendor's products plus further pre-selected components plugged on top.

Basis for the functional evaluation were the client's extensive requirements specifications that had been created to develop the intended bespoke solution from scratch. The classification of all requirements into 20 high level characteristics, or feature sets, were based on these requirements specifications and were created by the consultant together with the client. The final feature sets covered quite the complete range of business support that a large full-service communications provider needs. The consultant's experience and some theoretic suggestions from literature (Tam & Tummala 2001) complemented the requirements where it was necessary. To give an idea, the feature sets were for example payments management, workforce management, product and service management, etc.

The evaluation itself was based on a detailed questionnaire with roughly 1'200 single assessment items which were derived directly from the feature sets. The assessment items measured, within each feature set, if the requirements element in question was fulfilled by the examined solution, or not. The positive items inside a predefined feature set were counted and the percentage against all items in the feature set was calculated. In Figure II.R2-2, this overall percentage of fulfillment shown as distance from the center of the diagram, with the 20 feature sets shown as segments of the circle.

The survey was conducted by filling in the questionnaire for each of the five packages from the market plus the individual solution, and this examination was done for each of the six analyzed solutions and for each feature set. In Figure II.R2-2, the result of this evaluation is shown. The strong dashed line represents the functional scope of the individual development and the five thin lines each represent the functional scope of one package that could be procured on the market.

The largest difference between the best package from the market and the individual solution with a major discrepancy of 36 percentage points difference (feature set no. 11) was in disadvantage of the bespoke solution. The second largest difference (no. 18), with 22 percentage points from the leading market package, was again in disadvantage of the individual development. The third largest difference (no. 12), with 17 percentage points from the leading market package, was again in disadvantage of the individual development. Out of the 20 characteristics assessed, ten favoured one or the other package solution and six favoured the individual solution, with four draws. Depending on the actual metrics used for

comparison, the result can look a little different but is always in favour of the packages from
the market.

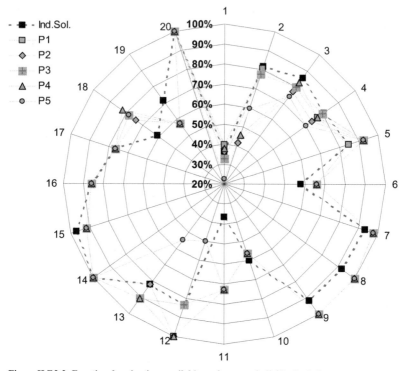

Figure II.R2-2: Functional evaluation, available packages vs. individual solution.

Note that the individual solution initially was expected to cover all feature sets extremely
well, since the feature sets were defined from the original requirements that also drove the
development of this very solution. Note further that the five package solutions represented
functionality that was actually available, while the individual solution was an unfinished work
in progress at the time of the analysis, and the recorded functionality was the system's
intended functionality once development work was completed. Against initial expectations,
this comparison indicated that the functionality of software packages from products and
components available on the market had a better fit with the client's requirements than the
bespoke solution developed specifically for these requirements.

Discussing the results of this functional evaluation, the client perceived the following core
topics as also influencing the decision:

Complexity. "Components tend to be complex because they implement many features, or because the features are difficult to implement properly, or both. Complexity arises from the fact that a component vendor must convince us that it is better to buy the component than it is to build it."

Dependency. "Producing high-quality implementations is an expensive and in business terms risky undertaking. It is obvious, then, that component vendors strive to make us depend upon their components to protect their revenues as we purchase software support and component upgrades. Thus components tend to be highly product-specific, and also the all-important task of integrating different components becomes more difficult."

Hyper-competition. "In the component industry successful features are quickly copied by competitors. This forces the original vendor to seek new ways to differentiate its component, leading to a new round of innovation, and so forth. The hyper-competitive nature of the component market made commercial software technology reach capabilities today that could only be dreamed of only few years ago. However, such pace of innovation ensures that whatever component competence we obtain is sure to become stale within surprisingly short time. Component competence, then a key organizational asset, wastes rapidly in a hyper-competitive environment."

Double constraints. "A fully integrated system made from available components is constrained twice: first by requirements of our end-users and second by capabilities of available components. Today it is almost certainly hopeless to assume that somewhere in the marketplace we find a collection of commercial products that happen to fit perfectly with our needs." This perception is interesting especially vs. the evidence of the functional evaluation.

Pragmatism. "Component evaluation has a new element of pragmatism. We assess requisite functional capabilities that we need, but we also look at what else the component might do. An unexpected and useful feature might lead us to reconsider the overall system design."

2.2 Integration scenario case studies

The consultant provided seven comparable case studies of renowned incumbents describing their choice between "Make" or "Buy" based integration. The consultant selected the different scenarios from references comparable with the client's situation.

Figure II.R2-3 shows the case studies, indicating the classification as development or procurement of software, a classification of the overall project success, and also the project size (symbolic). Three of the described cases were "Make" integration scenarios (A2, A3, A6) and four cases were "Buy" integration scenarios (A1, A4, A5, A7). Five of the projects reached the objectives (A1, A3, A5, A6, A7) and two did not (A2, A4). These case studies were intended to support a concrete client in an actual decision. They do not bear any statistical significance since they were no random sample but deliberately chosen to match with certain aspects of the client's situation. This means also that conclusions such as "bigger projects tend to fail more often" should not be drawn from the case studies.

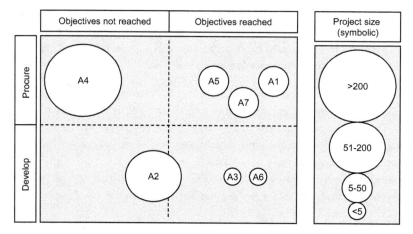

Figure II.R2-3: Seven case studies of software integration scenarios.

A1 had been chosen because the company had a very high number of IT staff in relation to the total number of employees. A1 integrated an externally procured system for business customers, introducing also the new business processes enabled by the new system in parallel. The "Buy" decisions were greatly based on the internal development units not being able to realize the project within the necessary time frame. The project succeeded but the original timing could not be kept, mainly due to migration problems from unexpectedly low source data quality and poor and missing documentation of the source systems.

A2 had been chosen because the company had approximately the size of the client in terms of employees and customers. The intended "Make" solution was based on the re-engineering and functional extension of an existing and inherited proprietary system. In A2, the new system went live at the deadline and worked successfully and error-free due to a sophisticated and elaborate testing from the very beginning. However, the system initially did not deliver its full functionality – in fact, significantly less functionality was available than in the old system before, making users truly unhappy. The intended functionality could only be realized in a number of follow-on releases.

A3 had been chosen because the intended individual solution was very similar to a part of the client's existing IT structure. The solution was built on individually developed software added up with few small externally procured and proprietary products. A3 objectives were mere technical, not functional, including a massive performance improvement of batch throughputs and online response times, and A3 succeeded with a "Make" approach on a very low budget. An extended plan of introducing at the same time functional extensions was blocked by IT management due to limited development resources internally and on supplier side.

A4 had been chosen because the company had a size and structure very similar to the client's. The intended integration in A4 was pure "Buy" with a mixture of products bought from different vendors. A4 tried to restructure the whole enterprise business procedures and integrate the related systems in parallel. The plan failed, even with massive additional external support. Transition and data migration took longer than ever expected. Essential knowledge went to external resources and put A4 in long-term supplier dependencies.

A5 had been chosen because the company had ambitious targets and was located in a cultural environment similar to the client's. Sixteen percent of the personnel were IT staff, and the "Buy" decision replaced an outdated system not any more maintained by the vendor. A5 delivered technically, and in particular the project managed to migrate the legal master data successfully. However, the TCO (total cost of ownership) quickly exceeded the initial software life cycle plan.

A6 had been chosen because it is a successful example for revamping the enterprise business procedures and at the same time integrating a new system that is able to handle the future processes. Ten percent of the company's staff were IT employees, and the "Make" decision included the plan for the software to be maintained and further developed also by external IT staff. However, this case was a comparatively small company, not a full communications portfolio provider as were the other examples.

A7 had been chosen because the company was in a very similar strategic and competitive situation. The "Buy" integration replaced several de-central legacy systems on scattered databases by one central software bought on the market. In parallel the IT organization structure was consolidated, too. The in-house organizations that had developed and maintained the previous systems were set to support the new product. A7 succeeded within the calculated CAPEX but exceeded the time frame by far – while the timing was not the top priority for A7.

For the support of the client's decision, discussions of the presented cases revealed certain of the client's perceptions:

- "Design focus shifts towards fitting pieces together rather than defining internal structures of single functions. No unit tests or inspections of packaged software, because it does not come with source code."

- "Interaction with vendors greatly increases and occurs at different levels throughout a project."

- "Procurement requires more technical knowledge so it is not a pure administrative activity, but technical personnel are often not prepared to deal with procurement issues."

- "Product evaluation becomes a core activity – but developers are not always prepared for it."

- "The amount of bought solutions drives different processes. A project that only uses one large procured package follows completely other processes as compared to an integration of numerous packages that will constitute most of the resulting system."

Discussing the case studies with the client, perceived advantages of "Buy" integration decisions were:

Flexibility: "There is usually some room to adjust requirements to fit the products being used." *Programming*: "Large portions of the system are constituted by a ready-made product and thus do not have to be written and debugged." *Life cycle*: "Possibly because of schedule pressure, 'Buy' integration projects seem to be completed more quickly." *Adherence to schedules*: "There is a perception that schedules are kept better in 'Buy' integration projects, although this cannot be confirmed empirically." *Useful functionality*: "Functionality is discovered in a package that was useful, even though the project had not originally planned to use it."

Discussing the case studies with the client, perceived disadvantages of "Buy" integration decisions were:

Knowledge: "Good or bad surprises having to do with the quality or functionality of a ready-made product." *Communication*: "The vendor constituted one more party with whom communication channels had to be established and maintained." *Dependencies*: "Project personnel had to rely on the vendor for a variety of mainly technical issues." *Negotiations*: "Technical personnel were not always prepared to deal with the business aspects of purchasing and managing a software product."

Further to the described points, practically all projects show that the success of integration depends mostly on the qualification of the involved people, on the actual project set-up and the financial and managerial backing – taking into consideration local culture and principles.

3   Conclusion and remarks

This experience report presented an extract from an IT strategy consulting in a situation that was mission critical for the client. The client requested decision support with a very large individual software development and integration project that had repeatedly failed to deliver. The client requested to propose the alternative of procuring and integrating respective software packages on the market, and to compare this alternative against the finalization of the ongoing individual development and integration. Several work areas were part of the consultation, and two of them were selected for this report and explained in more detail.

A functional comparison was made between the bespoke solution development and five packages assembled from products and components available on the market. Different from expectations, this comparison favoured the integration of package solutions. Further discussions with the client on this topic, specifically on compositional reuse, revealed some reluctance of the client against the component idea for perceived reasons of complexity, dependency, hyper-competition, double constraints and pragmatism.

Case studies that were relevant in certain aspects for the client's decision situation were selected, described and discussed with client management. On the bottom line, the cases studies gave an inconsistent picture for the integration decision and it was concluded that further key success factors, other than the question whether integration is driven by development or by composition, had a strong influence on the cases. The client recognized both pros and cons of the integration approaches, as well as the inconclusiveness of restricting the overall picture to that question.

In the presented report, the consultant's task was restricted to the alternative of full package integration only. Consequently, compositional solutions could only indirectly be included in the decision support, namely as parts of full packages. Otherwise, as visualized in Figure II.R2-1, a combination of large-scale and small-scale development, also in the sense of a "make and buy" approach (Kurbel et al. 1994), might have been a promising idea to assess.

References

Becker, S.; Overhage, S. (2003), "Stücklistenbasiertes Komponenten-Konfigurationsmanagement", *Tagungs-band 5. Workshop komponentenorientierte betriebliche Anwendungssysteme*, Gesellschaft für Informatik, 25-26 Feb. 2003, Augsburg: 17-32.

Biggerstaff, T.; Richter, C. (1987), "Reusability framework, assessment, and directions", *IEEE Software*, 4 (2): 41-49.

Ewers, J.; Jaekel, T.; Janson, M.; Skroch, O. (2004), "The impact of EU liberalization on telecommunication service providers in EU applicant countries", Detecon, Bonn.

Frost and Sullivan (2003), "World communication billing software market analysis", Frost and Sullivan, San Jose, USA.

Kurbel, K.; Rautenstrauch, C.; Opitz, B.; Scheuch, R. (1994), "From 'make or buy' to 'make and buy': Tailoring information systems through integration engineering", *Journal of Database Management*, 5 (3): 18-30.

McIlroy, M. (1969), "Mass produced software components", *Software engineering: Report on a conference sponsored by the NATO Science Committee*, NATO Scientific Affairs Division, 7-11 Oct. 1968, Garmisch: 138-155.

Mili, H.; Mili, F.; Mili, A. (1995), "Reusing software: Issues and research directions", *IEEE Transactions on Software Engineering*, 21 (6): 528-562.

Ortner, E. (1998), "Ein Multipfad-Vorgehensmodell für die Entwicklung von Informationssystemen – dargestellt am Beispiel von Workflow-Management Anwendungen", *Wirtschaftsinformatik*, 40 (4): 329-337.

Pyshkin, K. (2003), "Operator strategies and key performance indicator benchmarks", Analysys Research, Cambridge, UK.

Skroch, O.; Turowski, K. (2006), "Technische Grundlagen von Voice over IP", in Büllesbach, A.; Büchner, W. (eds), *IT doesn't matter!? – Aktuelle Herausforderungen des Technikrechts*, Schriftenreihe Informationstechnik und Recht der Deutschen Gesellschaft für Recht und Informatik, Volume 15, Otto Schmidt, Cologne: 17-32.

Szyperski, C. (1998), *Component software: Beyond object-oriented programming*, Addison Wesley, Harlow, UK.

Taubner, D. (2005), "Software-Industrialisierung", *Informatik Spektrum*, 28 (4): 292-296.

Turowski, K. (2003), *Fachkomponenten: Komponentenbasierte betriebliche Anwendungssysteme*, Shaker, Aachen.

Tam, M.; Tummala, R. (2001), "An application of the AHP in vendor selection of a telecommunications system", *Omega – The International Journal of Management Science*, 29 (2): 171-182.

III Specification

III.R3 The importance of requirements specifications for successful IT projects [3]

Today, information technology not only shapes inevitable parts of daily life in modern societies, but also counts for one of the most important success factors in business. By strengthening their own, unique selling propositions, enterprises can achieve particular competitive advantages on the market. IT must support these individual propositions, respectively enable them in the first place. In order to plan, procure, develop, and operate the corresponding IT solutions in today's efficient and divided value creation processes, the exact requirements for the solutions need to be specified as clearly as possible. All parties involved in the divided work – including, for instance, the principal contractor, end-users, computing centers, systems integrators or developers – profit from unambiguous and resilient agreements, which reduce the numerous project risks along steadily globalizing value creation chains.

Nonetheless, it is typical that important aspects remain unexplained between the involved parties in scope of work descriptions representing the technical contents of such (legal) agreements. Substantial tactical advantages for competition are thus wasted – or are even inverted when projects fail. The following research article identifies success factors which enable competitive advantages through high quality requirements specifications and scope of work descriptions in daily business practices. The article also illustrates risks associated with neglecting specification issues, including the worst case, the legal dispute. The article thus covers topical interdisciplinary questions at the interface between business informatics and law.

---

[3] Research article R3: Pruß, M.; Skroch, O. (2010), "Die Bedeutung der Anforderungsspezifikation für erfolgreiche IT-Projekte", *HMD – Praxis der Wirtschaftsinformatik*, 46 (272): 100-107.

1   Requirements specifications in the development process

Systematic development processes start with requirements which are set by principals as the decisive foundation and driver for further development activities. In divided value creation chains these requirements must be communicated between the involved players. Therefore, it needs to be clearly described first *what* exactly the issues are; in subsequent steps it becomes possible to work out *how* they can be solved later. High quality requirements specifications are needed to communicate the problem to be solved and drive the divided development work. Ideally, we could think of these specifications as standardized documents. In divided application software development work, such unambiguous specifications are a central prerequisite for the successful composition of large solutions from parts of diverse origin (Grollius, Lonthoff & Ortner 2007, pp. 40-42). These clear requirements specifications set the guaranteed properties of a desired solution in black box style "from the outside", at the interfaces between different system parts. They can then be legally agreed upon as the scope of work descriptions. Thus they are possibly the single most important key success factor in modern IT development processes (Gsell, Overhage & Turowski 2008, pp. 47f).

However, in day-to-day IT development practices we can see that the significance of requirements specifications has not been fully recognized yet by many decision makers in businesses or institutions. The quality of requirements specifications, therefore, often has an inferior role when developing, selecting, or introducing IT solutions. An examination of large IT projects in public administration has, for instance, identified difficulties with the specifications as one of the core problems; the largest of the investigated projects alone was estimated to have caused financial losses of roughly five billion Euro, inclusive of opportunity costs (Mertens 2009, p. 44, p. 46). Similar problems caused by specifications are regularly discovered in enterprises of all sizes. Just recently, a medium-sized engineering company, which produces tailor-made architectural glass wall units, purchased commercial off-the-shelf business support software for the glass construction business without a detailed requirements specification. Later it turned out that the software package could not support any of the specific work procedures required by the company for building their complex, individually tailored glass wall units at all. The project led to a legal slugfest.

2   Success factors

For the illustration of success factors for the creation of clear requirements specifications, we initially distinguish between the involved parties. The principal contractor in a typical IT project deals with many different participants, such as product manufacturers, consultants, systems integrators, quality assurance specialists, and others. Content-wise, the collaboration between the participants is determined by the agreed scope of work descriptions with the guaranteed system properties which emanate directly from the requirements specification. The following chapter looks at practical success factors for the principal when creating requirements specifications (Figure III.R3-1).

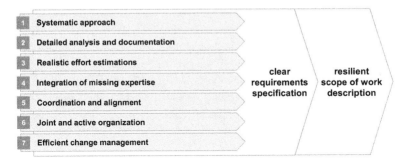

Figure III.R3-1: Success factors for clear requirements specifications.

2.1 Systematic approach

When preparing individually developed IT solutions, the development tasks thereby incurred can be mastered only with systematic approaches. Systematic technical development proceeds from requirements (*Lasten*) via design (*Pflichten*) towards realization and (acceptance-) testing. The single working phases and steps can be iterative, distributed, and complemented by accompanying tasks such as quality assurance or project controlling. Approaches that are actually used in practice usually differ from the development process models suggested in theory. They are, however, more successful if they are compliant with a systematic process. All involved players should, therefore, know these systematic process models and their meaning.

In particular when modeling requirements for software development, familiarity with semi-formal methods that are applied by experts from business informatics and software engineering is necessary. Examples of such methods include, among many others, the Event-driven Process Chain (EPC) or the Unified Modeling Language (UML).

In daily business practice, IT staff is often assigned requirements specification tasks irrespective of their actual qualification profiles. However, software development is quite different from tasks such as computing center operations or IT management. The IT department of a large specialized publisher, for example, cut down their own experts for software projects who worked on job descriptions such as systems analysts, project managers, etc. Hardly any internal knowledge of and experience with development tasks remained, particularly not for the analysis and documentation of individual requirements. Nevertheless, the IT department was still expected to produce respective deliverables – with little success though.

Configuration and parameterization for off-the-shelf software products initially must be distinguished from individual application software development. In complex IT products, however, parameter settings can become so challenging that this can only be controlled with systematic, development-like approaches, too. When purchasing commercial products, it is usually also necessary to make a choice from a number of eligible product alternatives. Ad hoc decisions will at best result in rare lucky strikes, but cannot systematically ensure a choice that optimally suits the actual requirements.

2.2   Detailed analysis and documentation

Once the central significance of his own requirements is recognized, this should motivate the principal to pay close attention to these requirements and their detailed documentation. The requirements should be collected on a sufficient level of detail, ideally according to a preset standard. Otherwise it can happen – as, for example, was the case in a large hospital – that engaged and trained people specify in great, nearly excessive detail while others work only very superficially.

Requirements specifications should be kept as simple as possible – but not any simpler. Experience shows that end-users often think that certain requirements, terms and definitions, procedures, etc. – namely those with which they are especially familiar – go without saying and do not specify them. Especially the behavior of currently used software tends to be implicitly supposed as self-evident to others, without plainly formulating what this behavior is. Experience has shown many cases with only one single requirement in the whole specification: abiding the laws. Such a simplification is often nurtured by the false implicit assumption that the characteristics of currently used software would be agreed in the scope of work without mentioning. However, the demand for accounting systems that conform to the laws and regulations, for example, has lead to a market with many different products and solutions that are all legally compliant. A certain product or solution is rendered more or less suitable for one's own actual set of requirements by its individual differences.

Requirements specifications can finally put forth scope of work descriptions as legally binding contractual agreements. These can become the technical basis for a legally relevant acceptance testing, too. Therefore, a first approximation for the suitable level of detail in scope of work descriptions is the possibility to create individual acceptance test cases. Ideally, the scope of work description even qualifies autonomously for the creation of software architecture and design, with minimum additional elicitation efforts in downstream development steps.

2.3 Realistic effort estimations

Even a specification of only the most relevant requirements can consist of many thousand single requirement items. The efforts which are associated with the creation of an individual document of this type and size are regularly underestimated in practice. An interesting example is an investment group which expected that all the requirements for the IT of a nationwide operating enterprise with a staff of several thousands could be documented in a legally binding way within three days.

Inappropriate evasion strategies must be avoided first and foremost. An often experienced evasion maneuver is the uncritical confidence that principals put in their suppliers, consultants, etc. Sometimes these agents suggest from a purely sales-related motivation to be familiar with all the issues and to have individually suitable solutions already. Their argument further reduces the principals' willingness to engage sufficiently in the identification of actual own requirements. But experience clearly shows that the individuality of each situation, enterprise, investment, or project issues ever new and unexpected challenges.

Another typical evasion maneuver is to request the creation of requirements specifications from employees in addition to other full time daily business tasks. However, analyzing and documenting individual requirements for development is a demanding and laborious work which, among other things, requires close concentration and intensive communication. Specifying requirements can hardly be successful when operated in a casual manner.

The high efforts associated with analyzing and documenting requirements are often discouraging. However, requirements specifications must not be evaluated only from the costs that are induced by their creation. With requirements specifications, as with any other investment or engagement, reasonable decisions are substantiated more broadly. Therefore, the benefits and value propositions of the requirements specification must also be considered, and the risks from the overall significance of the desired solution must be accounted for just as well. (DeMarco 1997, pp. 30-33).

2.4 Integration of missing expertise

In virtually all fields of engineering it is common practice to employ highly qualified experts when specifying requirements for complex products or comprehensive services which are being developed. In larger settings dedicated planning departments are routinely established. As experience shows, these expert planners need to be highly qualified. Apart from general methodical competences and knowledge of their own technical discipline (such as mechanical engineering or marketing), they also have to be specifically conversant with the target business (such as the automotive industry).

The software development area is commonly recognized as very challenging, hence it all the more needs well-grounded expertise and experience. Paradoxically, however, the involvement of professional specialists in software engineering is widely deemed to be less necessary as compared to other well-established engineering domains – although many players have asked for more understanding and higher professionalism for a long time.

2.5   Coordination and alignment

From all the single requirements that are specified in detail, one coherent and manageable overall package needs to be compiled. This demands an adequate and coordinated reconciliation between the stakeholders. Contradictions and gaps in the requirements have to be discovered and expensive requirements which generate little value but high costs have to be identified so that informed decisions can be taken. For instance, a department from a governmental institution of adult education demanded that their certifications should be made tamper-proof by including micro-printed elements. In an alignment review it turned out that the benefits of this requirement could not justify its high costs, as special paper types and printing equipment would be needed. Such exaggerated demands from certain stakeholders need to be identified and eliminated, otherwise they will appear in the scope of work description.

From experience this coordination and alignment factor also provides a good occasion to identify, based on the documented requirements, wrong or error-prone work procedures. Suitable measures can be taken and business processes can thus explicitly be aligned with requirements, or vice versa. This aspect is especially emphasized with the setup of service-oriented architectures.

Large requirements documents need to be consolidated to a well-aligned, coordinated, and clearly arranged requirements catalogue also to better perform a possible tendering process for correspondingly large projects and solutions later.

2.6   Joint and active organization

Even sufficient external expertise in requirements specification does not release the principals from their close cooperation. The involved participants must create the requirements specification as a team and collaborate closely and trustingly. External specialist usually do not know the individual, internal peculiarities demanded for a tailor-made solution, and internal partners and colleagues typically lack the profound technological and methodical expertise. Their joint activities need to be managed in an active and supporting manner. Otherwise, as experience has often shown, all kinds of surprises can appear at the end of this phase. However, it is the genuine and prime interest of all the involved players that a true common understanding is achieved as to the expected scope of work and that this understanding is unambiguously specified in a resilient and reviewable document.

A sad example is the mission-critical IT systems development project at a large infrastructure supplier. After several project years, still no tangible results were delivered at all. A due diligence was performed on the project and revealed that, among other things, no requirements had been specified and no current project planning existed. A project culture had emerged instead which made it nearly impossible to address or only mention any issues, or to call in decisions.

2.7   Efficient change management

Change management procedures for a software development project are often legally agreed upon in the related contracts. Such procedures, therefore, do not necessarily belong to the critical success factors for requirements specifications in the narrow sense. However, as large projects move on, it can become inevitable, even with high quality requirements specifications, to change the scope of work that had originally been agreed upon. The more the scope of work description is unclear and instable, the more debated points appear and need to be discussed in the change management procedure. The change management clauses – which originally have been foreseen as fallback for exceptional cases only – can become the standard mode of operation. As experience shows, sufficient resources are rarely planned for such a situation, which puts considerable additional load on a project. It has led, in many known cases, to the point where ongoing change management issues were preventing any further progress of the whole development. From a practical viewpoint, such a situation can hardly be brought to a successful or at least amicable outcome any more.

Therefore, the involvement of an unbiased professional who is accepted by all participants should be considered in change management procedures with deficient or unclear requirements specifications. This authority should be involved as early as possible as a precaution to avoid further delay in a critical situation. The authority can be empowered as a referee to take final decisions or can act as a mediator and make nonbinding proposals.

3   Risks

To illustrate the importance of high quality requirements specifications and unambiguous scope of work descriptions it is especially helpful to portray the risks that can arise from unclear, missing, or incomprehensible agreements (Figure III.R3-2).

These risks do not arise in modern IT development projects only. In the complex and divided development work in the information technology area, scope of work descriptions also occupy a most central role. So their deficiencies strongly aggravate the associated risks. The particular experiences with expert witness opinions at law courts show that players regularly fail to draw operational consequences even after recognizing the significance of clear scope of work descriptions in principle.

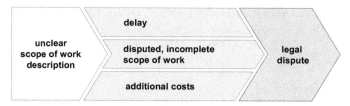

Figure III.R3-2: Risks from unclear scope of work descriptions.

3.1   Disputed and incomplete scope of work

Principals who initially devoted only little attention to their own actual requirements often have to recognize the absence of a true common understanding of the scope of work in the further course of a development project. This can happen in different project phases, depending on the process model chosen for the development. For conflicts identified early in a development cycle, alternative courses of action can often easily be negotiated. The later the differences are revealed in the course of the development, the more this becomes difficult though. Practical experience shows that hoping to still keep project goals, to clarify disputed issues, and to take missing decisions is often in vain at late development stages.

Experience also shows that principals keep on failing to recognize the significance of preparing their own expressive acceptance tests to check the actually delivered scope of work against the agreements. It is admittedly inefficient to prepare detailed acceptance test cases for each single requirement. It seems inevitable though to safeguard each business-critical requirement and to systematically prepare and execute respective acceptance test scenarios. For the traceability in a possible (legal) dispute, acceptance test results should even be reproducible to proof breaches in the delivered scope of work, or other identified defects, without any doubt. In practice, however, principals again and again have confidence in their agents even with regard to preparing and executing legally relevant acceptance tests. They simply trust in having received a complete, stable, and suited solution. It is only during live operation and with corresponding impacts that they learn about requirements that are not actually covered and about deficiencies that still exist.

A pleasant example is a communications network operator and service supplier who has operated very successful until today. This player recognized the meaning of (acceptance) testing for principals, consequently he took adequate care of the preparation of acceptance tests and set up a test lab in time. Among the competitors, this player thus was the only one to fully succeed in developing and integrating his own enterprise-wide business and operations support system. Nearly all the former competitors have vanished from the market today, and one of them was ruined by the direct consequences of the failed attempt to develop a similar solution.

3.2 Delay

Disputes about the scope of work usually cause considerable delays which emerge from the time and resources that have to be allocated to related discussions and negotiations. The more scope of work descriptions turn out to be ambiguous and instable, the more time and resources are needed for subsequent debates.

Each party must review those parts of the requirements specifications and scope of work descriptions that are interpreted differently by the different players. When negotiating amicable courses of action, proposed solutions and their consequences and alternatives have to be analyzed to assess if they are acceptable in each case. Buffer time for such processes was hardly planned before. In practice most decisions, in particular those of larger impact, also depend on certain individuals or institutions which are not always available. All things considered, delays of unpredictable duration can result.

Moreover, many projects are tied into hard external deadlines and schedules. Changed legal regulations, for instance, have to be implemented up to given deadlines. Other hard time limits are set by market necessities, for instance, related to the Christmas business. Under such circumstances, delay alone can lead to final project failure.

3.3 Additional costs

Even if certain scope of work areas were specified unclearly, or were not specified at all, the undocumented scope is usually required nonetheless. The missing specification parts then must be created ex post and the whole development project has to be extended. The related, additional efforts, though, have not been planned before. In practice, such efforts then come at unfavorable conditions as compared to efforts planned in advance and negotiated at the beginning of the overall project. Thus a pretended offer on easy terms can later still turn out worse in comparison.

Such cost explosions can be observed most clearly in certain very large development projects for correspondingly large principals, such as public administrations or global enterprises. These players often decide with long-term ranges of consideration and invest out of strategical, political, or similar concerns. They often consider it better to somehow continue instead of cancelling such a project. Hence such projects often need large raises in the budget and much additional time. It is often realized only too late that even long-term targets, even pursued with great dedication and resources all-out, still cannot be achieved if the intentions have been underestimated from the beginning and have been planned and implemented in an unprofessional manner.

3.4   Legal dispute

If no settlements can be reached either within the regulations of the agreed contracts or through negotiations between the involved parties, then the last escalation level is a legal dispute. This generates costs that have not been calculated by anyone beforehand. Moreover, the duration and result of a legal proceeding is hardly predictable, even with seemingly obvious claims and positions in the beginning.

Law courts in Germany regularly refer to *"Stand der Technik bei einem mittleren Ausführungsstandard"* (BGH 2003, p. 1) or to *"anerkannte Regeln der Technik"* (Bayerlein 2008, §16 marginal number 21) as the last way out of unclear scope of work descriptions. This approach may be sufficient in engineering disciplines where commonly accepted norms, regulations, and standards exist. However, the information technology area, and specifically the software domain, suffers from an excess of competing standards and technologies which exist in parallel but are neither commonly accepted nor generally used. In software engineering, for instance, not even a commonly accepted construction theory has been established by now. Therefore, the "state of technology" or an "average implementation standard" cannot be defined objectively. The state of technology is barely determined for the typical application areas and target domains in business informatics, too. Even the (lower) "accepted technical rules" can only be found in few and clearly separated target domains, such as in financial accounting.

Therefore, at court expert witnesses normally deliver their opinion, based on their personal experiences and market insights (Jäger et al. 2003, pp. 140-142). To a great deal the courts' sentences depend on these expert witnesses' opinions. As the expert witness is unbiased, his opinion will hardly be in accordance with the beliefs of the disputing parties. The importance of detailed and unequivocally interpreted requirements specifications will then become obvious to all parties at the latest.

4 Future requirements

Critical success factors promote the creation of clear requirements specifications. Neglecting these factors bears significant risks. In practice, specifying unambiguous requirements notoriously fails. Consequently, scope of work descriptions are rarely understood and interpreted in a common way and thus are not legally resilient in divided development work.

The importance of resilient scope of work descriptions that do not bear any unpredictable risks or legal issues as to their content further increases in two recent application software technology trends: service-oriented architectures / component- and service-orientation, and outsourcing / offshoring. Both approaches merely permit explicit dependencies at the interfaces between systems, applications, and organizations. These interfaces then must be considered in a purely formal manner in inter-organizational and inter-cultural relations. Virtually no assumptions can be made implicitly, and high quality, explicit requirements specifications and unequivocal scope of work descriptions gain their exceptional focal significance.

If the inevitable capacities for clearly specifying requirements are lacking, they have to be built up in the long term, and/or external resources have to be involved. High quality requirements specifications and contractually agreed, clear scope of work descriptions in the information technology and software sectors can then stipulate significant competitive advantages. This has been a matter of course for a long time already in similar, well established engineering disciplines.

References

Bayerlein, W. (2008), *Praxishandbuch Sachverständigenrecht*, 4th edn, Beck, Munich.

BGH (2003), Bundesgerichtshof, decision of 16 Dec. 2003, X ZR 129/01, accessed on 26 Jan. 2009, http://www.bundesgerichtshof.de.

DeMarco, T. (1997), *Warum ist Software so teuer? Und andere Rätsel des Informationszeitalters*, Hanser, Munich.

Grollius, T.; Lonthoff, J.; Ortner, E. (2007), "Softwareindustrialisierung durch Komponentenorientierung und Arbeitsteilung", *HMD – Praxis der Wirtschaftsinformatik*, 43 (256): 37-45.

Gsell, B.; Overhage, S.; Turowski, K. (2008), "Unzureichende Leistungsbeschreibung bei der Softwareentwicklung und die Rolle von Standardverträgen", in Möllers, T. (ed.), *Standardisierung durch Markt und Recht*, Nomos, Baden-Baden: 23-48.

Jäger, K.; Lenzer, J.; Scheider, J.; Wißner, B. (2003), *Begutachtung und rechtliche Bewertung von EDV-Mängeln*. Wißner-Verlag, Augsburg.

Mertens, P. (2009), "Schwierigkeiten mit IT-Projekten der öffentlichen Verwaltung", *Informatik-Spektrum*, 32 (1): 42-49.

III.R4   A method to evaluate the suitability of requirements specifications for offshore projects[4]

Globally distributing the development of information systems across organizational, national, and cultural borders increases the need for explicit understandings between the parties involved. This especially sharpens the focal significance of requirements specifications for communicating the development scope as explicitly as possible. The success of offshore steps in developing business application software therefore frequently depends on the quality of the respective requirements specifications. Often enough though, these specifications are not fully suitable for an offshoring context. The way in which their deficiencies are managed then becomes a key issue.

The following research article presents a method to evaluate the suitability of requirements specifications for an offshore application software development project. The method considers eight quality criteria and also five potentially compensating factors to balance out requirements specification deficiencies in the course of further development stages. The application of the method is illustrated in a case study hosted in an industry-size, prolific offshore IS development planning and decision support situation. In the study, we apply the method to broadly assess the adequacy of offshoring approaches, supporting the top management of a global industry leader in the automotive business. Based on the method, we evaluate requirements specifications as to their offshoring fitness. We also validate the observations made in the study by monitoring and reviewing the application of the method itself as well as the evaluation results against the actual project progress later.

---

[4] Research article R4: Overhage, S.; Skroch, O.; Turowski, K. (2010), "A method to evaluate the suitability of requirements specifications for offshore projects", *Business & Information Systems Engineering*, 2 (3): 155-164. © Gabler Verlag, Wiesbaden, Germany for the original contribution.

1   Motivation

Assigning the development and operation of information processing functions to external partners became a sustainable business model in 1963 at the latest, when the EDS company agreed with the Blue Cross health insurance to completely take over their IT (Dibbern et al. 2004, pp. 7f). Contracting out parts of business application development to external service providers has become a standard planning alternative today. For some time, the offshoring approach – outsourcing to low-wage areas that are envisaged to be far away and barely regulated ("off shore") – has been propagated in the course of globalization and has become the focus of considerations (Aspray, Mayadas & Vardi 2006, p. 6, p. 15; Kobitzsch, Rombach & Feldmann 2001, pp. 78-80; Pryor & Keane 2004, pp. 11-13).

On the contracting side, there primarily is the expectation of reducing costs through wage and price differentials between client and contractor areas. Aspray, Mayadas and Vardi (2006, pp. 6f) argue that economic theory as well as anecdotal evidence show economic benefits for clients and contractors. On the other hand, additional costs resulting from offshoring parts of the business application development are emphasized (Dibbern, Winkler & Heinzl 2008). Overby (2003, p. 65), for example, estimates that up to ten percent of additional costs incur for the necessary improvement of development processes only.

Today, offshoring is seen as a global mega trend (Boos et al. 2005, pp. 6f), and such approaches are now being pursued even for highly complex development projects. With the global allocation of development work to various stakeholders based on division of labor, the development task is directly subject to an inter-organizational and cross-cultural context where implicit assumptions can hardly be made (Hofstede 2002; Vlaar, van Fenema & Tiwari 2008, pp. 227-229; Winkler, Dibbern & Heinzl 2007, p. 96). Especially in such a context, necessary functions of an application system and required interfaces to other software components can only be explicitly specified through precise, intersubjectively unambiguous requirements specifications (Davis 1993). Therefore, requirements specifications constitute the substantive basis of the division of labor, become contractually agreed specifications of services (Gsell, Overhage & Turowski 2008, pp. 26-29; Overhage 2006, pp. 122-130), and are therefore one of the most important factors for offshore projects (Overby 2003, p. 65; Sakthivel 2007, p. 70).

Although precise requirements specifications are crucial and their quality has great influence on the results of subcontracted steps of application development (Wehrmann & Gull 2006, p. 407, pp. 413f), it is observed in practice that they routinely remain unclear and thus may create significant difference of opinion in regard to the agreed scope of services (Heindl & Biffl 2006, p. 21; Pruß & Skroch 2008; Vlaar, van Fenema & Tiwari 2008, p. 235). For a decision on the offshoring of developments steps, it is therefore essential to assess the suitability of requirements specifications in advance, e.g., based on criteria that have to be met. Despite the central importance of such an assessment, however, so far there have been hardly any efforts described to support this issue systematically and specifically with regard to offshore projects.

In this paper, we present a method to systematically and rationally assess the suitability of requirements specifications for the offshoring of development steps. The approach is characterized by two main features. First, the evaluation can be carried out without reconsulting users from the departments – who represent the requirements as regards content – for further clarification. In practice, such an approach would cause ongoing difficulties because of the users' limited availability and their limited willingness to discuss already given requirements again. Second, the approach's assessment also includes compensation opportunities, which makes it possible to (totally or partially) balance out specification deficiencies in a particular offshore project – these then constitute critical success factors for the offshore project to be carried out. For the preparation of appropriate sourcing activities, the presented approach not only makes it possible to assess a specification in terms of high or low quality. Additionally, it becomes possible to highlight compensating options for the responsible decision makers.

In developing the evaluation method, we followed the design-oriented approach of business and information systems engineering (BISE), specifically the design science method (Hevner et al. 2004). Apart from the theoretical foundation and iterative improvement, the latter also includes an explicit validation, which was primarily carried out in the context of a large case study. Here, the developed method was used in a large development project for custom software, providing decision support in the planning of the offshore parts of the project. The further presentation of the developed evaluation method is based on the design science cycle which differentiates between the formulation of the problem, the solution concept, the realization of the solution, and its validation as key steps (Takeda et al. 1990).

Section 2 describes the theoretical background and related approaches for the assessment of requirements specifications in order to highlight the existing research gap. Section 3 presents the conceptual basis of the evaluation method before it is presented in detail in Section 4. Section 5 includes a reflection of the performed case study as well as a reception of the results obtained. At the end of the contribution we discuss implications for science and practice as well as remaining research questions.

2   Background and related approaches

2.1   *Outsourcing, offshoring, and application development based on the division of labor*

The theoretical foundations of outsourcing have already been defined by Coase (1937, pp. 386-388) with his question about the limits of a firm, which among others served as a foundation for transaction cost economics. Along the value creation chain cost comparisons must determine whether subtasks are carried out internally or externally. Erber and Sayed-Ahmed (2005, p. 100) distinguish offshoring, inshoring, nearshoring, and onshore for the external processing. From the client's perspective, offshoring refers to the relocation of subtasks in areas far outside the national borders, while inshoring describes the same phenomenon from the contractor's perspective. In the case of nearshoring, client and contractor are located in close geographical proximity. Onshore means that both parties are located in the same country. Processes based on the division of labor can also be realized for business application development, which today generally is carried out starting from conception and analysis to cover design and finally also implementation and acceptance. The development can include iterative and distributed elements, and can be accompanied by various quality assurance measures, as described e.g. by Hansen and Neumann (2009, pp. 364-383).

Step	Conception	Analysis	Design	Implementation	Acceptance
Allocation	onshore	onshore	on-/offshore	on-/offshore	onshore
Starting Point	business goals	feasible targets	requirements specification	design	solution ready for acceptance
Core Activity	requirements analysis	requirements analysis	Architecture, planning	programming integration	testing
Core Deliverable	high-level requirements, feasibility	detailed requirements	design documents, detailed plans	completed application system	list of defects

Table III.R4-1: Process steps of application development (simplified).

Table III.R4-1 summarizes these typical, successive steps of application development each with their respective starting points, core activities, and results of the individual subtasks. At the end of each process step, the results should be documented in order to be used in subsequent steps. To emphasize the decision situation supported by the evaluation method, additional assumptions are made about the preconceived allocation options of individual development steps. Here, a decision on an offshore realization is envisaged for the design and/or implementation. Similar scenarios are also used by e.g. Boos et al. (2005, p. 25), Cusick and Prasad (2006, pp. 22f), or King and Torkzadeh (2008, pp. 209-212) for the discussion of offshoring approaches.

2.2   The importance of requirements specifications for offshoring

In their case study, Vlaar, van Fenema and Tiwari (2008, pp. 227-235) describe in detail the misunderstandings that may occur between a client's team that is responsible for the requirements analysis and the design, and an implementing team of the offshore contractor. Vlaar, van Fenema and Tiwari (2008, p. 235) summarize that "offshore team members could only develop literal understanding of the requirements" and thus point out how difficult it is to achieve an intersubjectively shared understanding of requirements in offshore projects. They explain that problems particularly result from "knowledge and experience asymmetries" as well as from "complex, novel and instable tasks and requirements" (Vlaar, van Fenema & Tiwari 2008, p. 242). From their argument that "requirements development is a fundamentally human-oriented and socially mediated process in which understandings are socially constructed" (Vlaar, van Fenema & Tiwari 2008, p. 239) it becomes clear that in the case of the offshoring of development steps additional difficulties in the already complex process of specifying requirements occur. "The ability to write clear specifications" is consequentially identified by Overby (2003, p. 65) as a key factor in the outsourcing of development tasks. Moreover, Wehrmann and Gull (2006, p. 407, pp. 413f) argue that uncertainties in the requirements have a strongly negative impact on offshoring. In a study of distributed development projects Heindl and Biffl (2006, p. 21) show that the highest risks result from "misinterpretation and unclear rationale of requirements". The quality of requirements specifications is therefore an essential risk factor for offshore projects (Sakthivel 2007, p. 70).

2.3   Evaluation approaches for requirements specifications

Although the assessment of the suitability of requirements specifications thus has a central relevance for the decision on offshoring development steps, few methods have been described by now which systematically support this task. In practice, the quality of large specification documents is often ensured ad hoc, little systematically, and with high human efforts. Most theoretical work, however, is devoted to the creation of formally correct specifications which can hardly be applied in practice. Scheffczyk et al. (2004, pp. 2-8) describe a commercially used method, which seeks to master this balancing act. Regarding the content, however, a substantive assurance of the requirements' consistency cannot be found here.

From the realm of experiences in a multinational conglomerate, Berenbach and Borotto (2006, pp. 448f) describe seven quality metrics used in UML (Unified Modeling Language) modeling. However, these again only cover the formal correctness of requirements and state nothing about their suitability as regards content. While in this approach every specification needs to meet the previously defined formal requirements, such a view is not sufficient for supporting a decision on an offshore project. In fact, a requirements specification in the terms of the approach by Berenbach and Borotto (2006, p. 446) could be complete even though requirements are missing (e.g. because they have not been modeled at all). For a comprehensive statement on quality, this relatively simple, formal verification therefore has to be supplemented by a more difficult validation as regards content.

Krogstie (1998, pp. 86-90) proposes an integrated framework for the quality assessment of requirements specifications, building upon the author's previous work and referring to the semiotic model by Morris (1970, pp. 13-42). The author shows that some of the classically discussed quality attributes, such as uniqueness of a specification, involve the dilemma that they can only be determined when the domain to be modeled is intersubjectively understood in a clear way already in advance (Krogstie 1998, p. 88, pp. 90f). This understanding, however, is to be attained through the specification process that otherwise would only be of documentary significance. In this way the quality framework addresses many quality attributes, but it remains too abstract for the actual application.

Wehrmann and Gull (2006, p. 407) suggest a complex cost estimation approach for the application development in offshore projects. They note that focusing on wage differences provokes miscalculation and that cost advantages rather depend on high-quality product requirements. In contrast, uncertainties of the requirements have a highly negative impact on the expected cost advantage, which cannot be further quantified with their method however. Dibbern, Winkler and Heinzl (2008, pp. 336-338) provide a model to explain costs in offshore projects. While they classify specification costs as crucial in the way that they should be included as one of five exogenous model variables, an evaluation of the suitability of a requirements specification for an offshore project is again not supported by their explanatory model.

Taking the mentioned works into account, in the next sections we describe, deploy, and validate a method which makes it possible to systematically verify the quality of documented requirements and their suitability for offshore development steps. The method intends to close the existing research gap and contribute to ensure that decisions about offshore projects can be based on a more comprehensive foundation in practice.

3   Conceptual basics

Requirements that are documented in a specification form the basis of and constitute the drivers for further development steps. They describe the functionality to be provided by an application system under certain conditions in the most precise and implementation-independent form based on the "externally" observable behavior of the application. Thus, they indicate *what* an application system performs without dwelling on *how* this is achieved (Liskov and Berzins 1986).

A declining *specification quality* usually leads to a higher interpretability for a third party as regards the content of the existing requirements. Hereby, direct implementation risks for the offshoring of later development steps are generated (Figure III.R4-1) which can be specifically balanced out by *compensating factors*. The lower the quality of the requirements specification, the higher is the risk that the necessary compensation cannot be afforded in subsequent development steps so that the quality of the implemented application system is impaired.

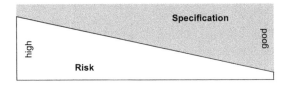

Figure III.R4-1: Relation between the specification quality and implementation risks.

Thus, in addition to the specification quality we also have to consider possible compensating factors through which existing specification gaps can possibly be balanced out when assessing the suitability of a requirements specification for an offshore project. Through such a sophisticated evaluation an additional scope for action results when deciding on an offshore project, which bears importance for practice. There, we can assume on the one hand just for economic reasons that complex requirements specifications cannot be arbitrarily improved after a potentially negative assessment. On the other hand, a development project has to deliver on its scope in the given time whilst adhering to budget constraints. Therefore, the method for the evaluation of requirements specifications proposed in this paper also explores alternative measures which may achieve a compensation of specification deficiencies that no longer can be overcome economically in an offshore project. Decision makers then can assess whether and how the compensation effort of an offshore project makes sense in a situational context despite existing specification deficits. However, the actions recommended as compensating factors then constitute critical success factors.

3.1   Specification quality

To assess how well a requirements specification is suited for the outsourcing of development work we generally have to consider different quality criteria. After evaluating the relevant literature, we used eight criteria for the evaluation method presented in this paper. These criteria were already used by the authors to evaluate specification approaches for development scenarios based on division of labor (Overhage 2006; Overhage & Thomas 2005). Overall, the following quality criteria of requirements specifications are to be assessed (Becker, Rosemann & Schütte 1995, pp. 437-439; Brown 2000, pp. 102f; D'Souza & Wills 1999, p. 321; Davis

1993, pp. 181f; Hall 1990, pp. 16f; IEEE 1998, pp. 4-8; Liskov & Berzins 1986, p. 3; Schienmann 1997, p. 26):

- q_1 *consistency*. The specification is supposed to clarify the relations between their individual components and to avoid contradictions between different parts of the specification in particular.

- q_2 *adequacy*. The outside view of the software should be described with reasonable efforts and at the same time in the highest possible precision – in particular, in a way that design and implementation tasks can be carried out with the specifications.

- q_3 *feasibility*. The specification should make use of notations established in practice that can be used effectively by all parties involved in the development.

- q_4 *flexibility*. The specification should have a uniform and modular structure so that requirements can be changed locally, if necessary.

- q_5 *standardization*. The specification should comply with mandatory, explicitly documented standards and guidelines concerning form and content.

- q_6 *comprehensibility*. Both the machine interpretability and the readability for people should be given. This means that on the one hand formal notations with precise syntax and semantics should be used, which on the other hand should also be presented in an easily understandable form with additional comments.

- q_7 *completeness*. All features of the application should be set in a way that makes it possible to conduct further development work on this basis. Completeness is required relatively, for example in terms of support for each specified task.

- q_8 *neutrality*. The specification should be independent of technologies and methods for the further development (design, programming, etc.).

To assess the above mentioned quality criteria in a decision situation they must be further operationalized and supplemented by concretely measurable dimensions. This is dependent on the context, such as for example on the specification methods. Therefore, it generally has to be performed according to situational peculiarities. As part of the case study discussed later, this contribution shows how the criteria were actually used there. For more information on the concrete terms of the above criteria the reader is referred to the relevant literature (IEEE 1998, pp. 4-8; van Lamsweerde 2009, pp. 87-90, pp. 187-189).

3.2   Compensation factors

Existing specification deficits may be compensated or at least controlled by specific measures during the offshoring project. In order to determine which compensating factors can be used specifically in such projects, we evaluated reviews and case studies on offshoring, outsourcing, and distributed application development. The analyzed works describe options for action that allowed the compensation of specification deficits completely or in parts. The relevant factors include the respective offshore partner's characteristics and possibilities of cooperation, but also the contractual design of the project.

Compensation	*domain knowledge*	*communication, language, and culture*	*learning relationship*	*reliability*	*contracting*
	e_1	e_2	e_3	e_4	e_5
Bhat, Mayank and Murthy (2006)		X	x	X	
Boos et al. (2005)	x	X	x	x	x
Corriveau (2007)					x
Davenport (2004)	x	X			
Gefen, Wyss and Lichtenstein (2008)	x		x		x
Heeks et al. (2001)	x	X	x		
Kojima and Kojima (2007)	x	X	x	x	x
Lacity and Willcocks (2003)				x	
MacGregor, Hsieh and Kruchten (2005)		X			
Moczadlo (2002)		X	x		
Nevo, Wade and Cook (2006)	x	X		x	
Remus and Wiener (2009)	x	X	x	x	x
Sakthivel (2007)			x		x
Setamanit and Raffo (2008)		X	x		
Siakas, Maoutsidis and Siakas (2006)			x	x	
Steimle (2007)		X	x	x	x
Tsuji et al. (2007)	x	X	x	x	x
Vlaar, van Fenema and Tiwari (2008)	x	X	x		
Wada, Nakahigashi and Tsuji (2007)	x	X	x	X	x
Winkler, Dibbern and Heinzl (2007)		X	x	X	

Table III.R4-2: Compilation of compensating factors in offshore projects.

The options for action are summarized in five compensating factors for decision makers in offshore projects in Table III.R4-2. References that discuss all the collected compensating factors are highlighted. In the context of each project therefore an investigation is necessary whether a situational compensation for specification deficits seems attainable through the observance of these compensating factors when selecting an offshore partner. The following factors are to be analyzed:

- e_1 *domain knowledge.* To what extent does the offshore partner have in-depth experience with similar requirements in general, and thus already possesses an implicit understanding of the application domain?

- e_2 *communication, language, and culture.* How easy or difficult is the operational communication between the offshore partners, in particular directly and personally?

- e_3 *learning relationship.* How mutually familiar are the respective partners with the people, the business, and the processes of the counterparts?

- e_4 *reliability.* What is the strategic interest or business model of the offshore partners? How qualified and motivated are the operational teams?

- e_5 *contracting.* How does the contract support detailing, clarification, and possible amendment of guaranteed characteristics in the course of the development project?

In most references, factor e_2 is not mentioned as a single factor. However, it makes sense to consider communication, language, and culture in context as is done here (Christiansen 2007, p. 25; Hofstede 2002).

4   Design of the evaluation method

The quality criteria and compensating factors form the basis for the rational evaluation method, i.e. a method that is transparent for the decision maker and is well founded in relation to the approach. As a key element we employ the cost-utility analysis approach that was introduced by Zangemeister (1976) for the multidimensional assessment and selection of project alternatives, and represents a proven method for decision making today (Klein and Scholl 2004, p. 87).

4.1   Procedure for determining the specification quality

To determine the quality of a requirements specification we classify this specification against each of the eight criteria presented q_i ($i = 1, ..., 8$) on a four-stage rating scale. On the scale, higher values express better suitability (Figure III.R4-2).

Depending on the specific project and the preferences of decision makers, each quality criterion can be optionally fitted with a weight g_i ($i = 1, ..., 8$). The overall assessment Q of the specification is the calculated by

$$Q = \frac{1}{8}\sum_{i=1}^{8} g_i q_i \text{ with } q_i \in \{1,2,3,4\}.$$
(III.R4-1)

Without an explicit definition of weights, all criteria are rated with an equal weight during the evaluation, thus $g_i = 1 \forall i$ holds. In case of an explicit weighting an appropriate normalization of g_i can be recommended, for example such that $\sum_{i=1}^{8} g_i = 8$.

The evaluation of the specification quality for each q_i is carried out individually and qualitatively by classification from the decision makers. Here, it is first determined whether the specification quality is in the upper ("above average or better") or lower ("below average or worse") range. Then the classification is refined and it is determined whether the specification within the upper range is thoroughly rated as "good" or only as "above average". Accordingly, one proceeds within the lower range, so that an overall range between 1 (worst) and 4 (best) results (Figure III.R4-2).

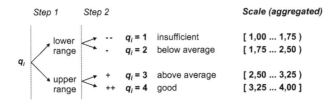

Figure III.R4-2: Two-stage, qualitative evaluation process to determine q_i.

Before the rating can be carried out, the specifications initially have to be analyzed by experts. The variety of the quality criteria to be assessed on the one hand intends to ensure the broadest possible analysis of specification documents. On the other hand, the evaluation generates additional efforts that should be limited by appropriate analytical techniques (e.g. sampling or clustering). One possible approach for this purpose is described later using the example case. The overall assessment which results from the application of the value analysis describes the quality of the specification.

4.2 Procedure for determining the compensation options

If specification deficiencies have been identified, we individually and qualitatively analyze for each of the impaired quality criteria q_i ($i = 1, ..., 8$) whether a balancing effect $k_{ij} \in \{0; 1\}$ can be expected in the project situation through the previously described compensating factors e_{ij}

($j = 1, ..., 5$), ($k_{ij} = 0$ for no, $k_{ij} = 1$ for yes). The balancing effects of the compensating factors in relation to the quality criteria is shown by the compensation matrix

$$k = (k_{ij}) = \begin{pmatrix} k_{11} & \cdots & k_{15} \\ \vdots & \ddots & \vdots \\ k_{81} & \cdots & k_{85} \end{pmatrix} \text{ with } i = 1,...,8; \ j = 1,...,5; \ k_{ji} \in \{0,1\}. \tag{III.R4-2}$$

The vertical compensation vectors $\vec{k}_{i1}^{\,V} = (k_{11}, k_{21}, \cdots, k_{81})$ to $\vec{k}_{i5}^{\,V} = (k_{15}, k_{25}, \cdots, k_{85})$ indicate which quality criteria are influenced by one compensating factor. The horizontal compensation vectors $\vec{k}_{1j}^{\,H} = (k_{11}, k_{12}, \cdots, k_{15})$ to $\vec{k}_{8j}^{\,H} = (k_{81}, k_{82}, \cdots, k_{85})$ show what factors effect a compensation for one quality criterion.

Quality Criteria	Success Factor				
	e_1	e_2	e_3	e_4	e_5
q_1	↵	↵			
q_2			↵	↵	↵
q_3		↵			
q_4	↵				
q_5	↵	↵			
q_6			↵		↵
q_7	↵				
q_8		↵			

Table III.R4-3: Graphical representation of expected compensation efforts (example).

Starting point for the compensation effort is the search for factors that at least partly enable compensating quality deficiencies in the requirements specification. The proposed analysis therefore focuses on the determination of the vertical compensation vectors. It pursues the question of what compensating effect can be expected from the various factors in the specific project situation (Table III.R4-3). In the style of the min-max-principle, according to which the maximum negative consequences are to be minimized, we aim at a compensation especially for the lowest-rated quality criteria of a requirements specification.

4.3 Further refinement of the evaluation

In the proposed approach for assessing requirements specifications, a lower quality measure implies a lower suitability of a requirements specification for the offshoring of development steps. It is also assumed that the suitability of a deficiency-afflicted specification is increased if effective compensating factors can be identified. For the assessment of the suitability we can supplement the condensed measure, which has been determined by the cost-utility analysis, by further analyses. Given the ordinal nature of the four-step scale, the measure allows the classification of the specification quality (Figure III.R4-2). However, it is not possible to make absolute statements and refer to specifications that are e.g. "twice as good" in comparison to others. Furthermore, the condensed measure alone implies that poor ratings of a quality criterion may be balanced out by good ratings of another one.

The further differentiation of the analysis may, for example, be performed using so called radar charts (Bensberg 2008), where in particular the possible compensating factors are to be integrated. Moreover, the assessment of individual criteria and their weights can be varied e.g. in the course of a sensitivity analysis. This allows an analysis to what extent the assessment depends on the suitability of the input variables, and thus how stable the results are. For the evaluation of the results of a cost-utility analysis as well as for supporting software tools, literature provides further reference (Bensberg 2008; Klein and Scholl 2004, p. 47).

5   Evaluation

The proposed evaluation method has been used in a case study that was hosted at a leading corporation in the automotive business. The suitability of extensive requirements specifications (including around 700 UML use cases) for the offshoring of further development steps had to be examined for one large development project. The purpose of the project was the development of an individually specified, complex and business-critical application system for the support and automation of the group's global sales processes. The application system should, among other things, provide the customized configuration of industrially produced technical capital goods and high quality consumer products for the global market. In the large development project the budgeted number of days of work for the preparation of requirements specifications by the client's internal employees alone amounted to a figure in the middle four digits. At the beginning of the case study, the specification of the requirements had been completed. The further project plan was to transfer large parts of the design and implementation to an offshore partner. The assessment of the requirements specifications began after the project management had approved the use of the presented evaluation method. The approach was conducted by an evaluation team including the authors of this contribution and representatives of the project leaders.

5.1   Determination of the specification quality

To determine the q_i, in a first step all cross relations between the parts of the specification were investigated for inconsistencies, contradictions, gaps, redundancies, lack of specification parts, and missing or incorrect identifiers. In a second step this was followed by a detailed examination of the requirements specifications' key parts which had been identified as "central" by the contracting body. For cost reasons, this investigation was partially restricted to a representative part of the specifications using a Pareto analysis (also known as "ABC analysis"). To implement the Pareto analysis, the previously analyzed cross relations were evaluated to draw conclusions about the relationship between the various parts of the specification. The part of the requirements specification classified as representative included, among others, 22 percent of the "central" use cases.

The evaluation of the specification parts was initially carried out by a verification against internal rules of the client and – where applicable – against formal rules, such as those of the UML. In addition, a validation was carried out by determining the requirements details that were missing to unequivocally work out a design. Any scope for discretionary interpretation that could not be removed by the requirements specifications was considered as a deficit here. The results formed the basis for the determination of q_i through a qualitative, consensus-based classification on the scale (Figure III.R4-2) by the evaluation team. Starting with the lowest-rated criteria the following assessments resulted (described in a very shortened way):

- q_1 *consistency*: 1 (--).-). A higher-level specification structure to explain the relations between parts of the specification was not available. The structure of the whole system was not sufficiently clear.

- q_2 *adequacy*: 1 (--).Due to the lack of precision of most of the requirements it was not possible to create a design of the application without additional elicitation.

- q_4 *flexibility*: 1 (--).The specification parts were heavily dependent on one another; these dependencies were not well described.

- q_6 *comprehensibility*: 2 (-).Large parts of the requirements specification were modeled in a semi-formal specification language (UML). However, the reference to complementary natural language parts of the specification remained blurred.

- q_7 *completeness*: 2 (-).It was noted that specification parts that are relevant for the further development were described only incompletely or as placeholders.

- q_3 *feasibility*: 3 (+).The notations used in the analyzed parts of the specification are commonly used in practice. Some techniques, however, were specific to the client.

- q_5 *standardization*: 3 (+). In general, the explicit and implicit violations of standards and guidelines were low in general.

- q_8 *neutrality*: 4 (++). The specification was described independently of technologies and methods for further development.

The investigation of the requirements specification revealed a total calculative value of 2.125 using (III.R4-1), and thus was below the average rating of the scale (Figure III.R4-2). In three of the eight quality criteria, the specification was classified as inadequate.

5.2 Determination of the compensation possibilities and options for actions

To assess the suitability of the requirements specification for the offshoring of further development steps more comprehensively, possible compensating factors for the identified specification deficiencies were examined and discussed.

By consensus, the evaluation team determined for each compensating factor whether this factor can be expected to have a balancing effect, particularly on the characteristics classified as inadequate in this specific development situation (Table III.R4-4).

	Success factor				
Quality criteria that has been assessed as low	e_1 domain knowledge	e_2 communication, language and culture	e_3 learning relationship	e_4 reliability	e_5 contracting
q_1 consistent		↩	↩		
q_2 adequate	↩	↩	↩	↩	↩
q_4 flexible		↩	↩	↩	↩

Table III.R4-4: Identified compensating factors and balancing effects.

During the analysis, the following vertical compensation vectors were determined based on the observations and recommendations (simplified description):

- e_1 *domain knowledge*: $\vec{k}_{i1}^{V} = (0,1,k_{31},0,k_{51},k_{61},k_{71},k_{81})$. The unclear overall structure of the specification can hardly be compensated by a good general understanding of the application domain. However, development partners with better domain knowledge can render single interpretable specification parts more precise, with relatively low risk. If specification parts are not designed for changeability in advance, they can hardly be adjusted by good domain knowledge alone.

- e_2 *communication, language, and culture*: $\vec{k}_{i2}^{V} = (1,1,k_{32},1,k_{52},k_{62},k_{72},k_{82})$. The explicit information about dependencies between parts of the specification should be supported by good communication. A common language and smooth operational communication are among the basic requirements for the further use of specifications with substantive deficiencies. In the case of specifications that are difficult or laborious to change, the solution identification for necessary modifications is simplified if the conflict cultures of the involved partners are compatible.

- e_3 *learning relationship*: $\vec{k}_{i3}^{V} = (1,1,k_{33},1,k_{53},k_{63},k_{73},k_{83})$. Existing knowledge of the business context through experiences from earlier collaborations between the involved parties facilitates problem solving for insufficiently concerted specification parts. The experience curve of the learning relationship simplifies the clarification of inaccurately specified requirements. If partners are already familiar with mutual peculiarities and implications, even specifications that require high efforts for changing may be adapted with relative efficiency.

- e_4 *reliability:* $\vec{k}_{i4}^{V} = (0,1,k_{34},1,k_{54},k_{64},k_{74},k_{84})$. Operational collaboration and strategic ties between the partners have little influence on the degree of coordination between specification parts. A high degree of reliability between the partners, however, makes it possible to better adjust inaccuracies in the requirements specification. In the case of a strategically committed management and an operationally reliable interaction between the development team members, changes to poorly modifiable specifications become more feasible.

- e_5 *contracting:* $\vec{k}_{i5}^{V} = (0,1,k_{35},1,k_{55},k_{65},k_{75},k_{85})$. It does not seem plausible that specification parts should be better coordinated as a result of a flexible contract. However, the appropriate contract design is a precondition of being prepared for dealing with imprecise or unstable specifications and of effectively handling such situations externally. Good contracts can show possible solutions especially for those specifications that can only be modified with high expense.

In determining the compensation vectors particularly the possible balancing effects for the mostly affected quality criteria were examined, following the min-max principle. The analysis yielded an overall critical assessment of the suitability of the requirements specification for an offshoring of later development stages. To support decisions in favor of an offshore project, it was recommended to pay attention to the feasibility of the above described compensating factors when selecting partners and designing the project.

5.3   Reception of the results

The client decided to implement an offshore project, waived a targeted implementation of compensatory measures but, given the evaluation results, limited the offshoring rate to a maximum of 40 percent of the project. After some time, we were able to analyze the project's progress and survey the client on the project results as well as on his assessment of the evaluation method during a retrospective interview.

The part of the project that has been conducted offshore was referred to as problematic. About 25 percent of the developed functionality had to be redeveloped completely; another 25 to 50 percent had to be partially revised. Overall, less than half of the offshore developments remained without rework. One reason given was the missing familiarity of the contractor with the individual peculiarities on the client side. Since neither in-depth knowledge of the application domain existed nor common experience from previous projects was available, the contractor could only compensate existing specification deficits at great expense. The unclear contract design in terms of compensation for deficits also led to discussions about who should bear the responsibility for problems in dealing with requirements specifications.

The offshore quota in the correction of defects and in change requests was reduced to zero in the later project. The entire offshore rate for the whole project finally was below 10 percent. The client estimated an unspecific "offshoring advantage" of only 10–15 percent on the bottom line. The client further stated that offshoring on the basis of poor requirements specifications works with largely standardized and generally known features and processes at best – but is badly suited for the implementation of individual and highly specific features as in the examined project. The method we used to evaluate the requirements specifications, and our analyzed compensation factors, were generally appraised by the client as "all together correct and relevant". The evaluation results and predictions could also be verified in detail by the actual course of the project, specifically through analyzing the issues that occurred as a consequence of neglecting the compensation measures. These concrete results from the evaluation method and the compensation recommendations were assertively confirmed as correct by the client also in the retrospective interview.

6   Conclusion

With the growing importance of offshoring as a decision option even for highly complex application development projects, the quality of requirements specifications has evolved to a central determinant. In this contribution we therefore described a method to evaluate the quality of requirements specifications systematically, comprehensively with regard to several criteria, and in a rational process. In addition, compensating factors were included into the analysis to achieve a better control or even a rectification of specification deficits during the course of the project. The evaluation method does not require a renewed involvement of the user. In the case study, the assessment also accounted for only about four percent of the total expense which the client had estimated for the design and implementation on the basis of a function point analysis.

The presented research results have implications for both science and practice. For practice, the developed approach provides an immediately deployable, efficient way to constitute a better foundation for planning decisions for an offshoring project depending on the quality of available requirements documents. From a scientific point of view, the presented approach closed the research gap concerning decision support approaches for the planning of offshore projects for application development. To achieve a more comprehensive decision support in the planning of offshore projects, we particularly have to research further influencing factors. The method described in this paper presents a first step which was developed in terms of a design science approach and which has been iteratively improved. We focused on the quality of requirements specifications and specific compensating factors with a balancing effect on specification deficits.

The presented method itself is subject to further research to be carried out in further iterations of the design science cycle. On the one hand, focus is on the development of an algorithmic process to systematically derive the weights of the single quality criteria during the assessment based on the preferences of decision makers. The Analytic Hierarchy Process (AHP) serves as the basis for this purpose. On the other hand, we plan to develop best practices and guidelines for the application of the presented method through further case studies in collaboration with practice partners. In this way, we intend to further improve the desired offshore decision support.

References

Aspray, W.; Mayadas, F.; Vardi, M. (eds) (2006), "Globalization and offshoring of software: A report of the ACM job migration task force: The executive summary, findings, and overview of a comprehensive ACM report on the offshoring of software worldwide", ACM, New York, USA.

Becker, J.; Rosemann, M.; Schütte, R. (1995), "Grundsätze ordnungsgemäßer Modellierung", *Wirtschaftsinformatik*, 37 (5): 435-445.

Bensberg, F. (2008), "Nutzwertanalyse", in Kurbel, K.; Becker, J.; Gronau, N.; Sinz, E.; Suhl, L. (eds) (2008), Enzyklopädie der Wirtschaftsinformatik – Online-Lexikon, Oldenbourg. Munich.

Berenbach, B.; Borotto, G. (2006), "Metrics for model driven requirements development", *Proceedings of the 28th international conference on software engineering*, ACM, 20-28 May 2006, Shanghai, China: 445-451.

Bhat, J.; Mayank, G.; Murthy, S. (2006), "Overcoming requirements engineering challenges: Lessons from offshore outsourcing", *IEEE Software*, 23 (5): 38–44.

Boos, E.; Iesalnieks, J.; Keller, F.; Moczadlo, R.; Rathgeb, K.; Rohlfes, M.; Schmidt, C.; Stimmer, J. (2005), *Leitfaden Offshoring*, Bundesverband Informationswirtschaft, Telekommunikation und neue Medien e.V., Berlin.

Brown, A. (2000), *Large-scale, component-based development*, Prentice Hall, Upper Saddle River, USA.

Christiansen, H. (2007), "Meeting the challenge of communication in offshore software development", *Proceedings of the first international conference on software engineering approaches for offshore and outsourced development*, Lecture Notes in Computer Science 4716, Springer, 5-7 Feb. 2007, Zurich, Switzerland: 19-26.

Coase. R. (1937), "The nature of the firm", *Economica*, 4 (16): 386–405.

Corriveau, J. (2007), "Testable requirements for offshore outsourcing", *Proceedings of the first international conference on software engineering approaches for offshore and outsourced development*, Lecture Notes in Computer Science 4716, Springer, 5-7 Feb. 2007, Zurich, Switzerland: 27–43.

Cusick, J.; Prasad, A. (2006), "A practical management and engineering approach to offshore collaboration", *IEEE Software*, 23 (5): 20-29.

D'Souza, D.; Wills, A. (1999), *Objects, components, and frameworks with UML: The catalysis approach*, Addison Wesley, Upper Saddle River, USA.

Davenport, T. (2004), "What stays and what goes? Sourcing processes and jobs in the global economy", *Offshore oursourcing - risks and rewards: Symposium conclusions paper*, CFO Publishing, 17 Jun. 2004, New York, USA: 3–4.

Davis, A. (1993), *Software requirements: Objects, functions, and states*, Prentice Hall, Englewood Cliffs, USA.

Dibbern, J.; Goles, T.; Hirschheim, R.; Jayatilaka, B. (2004), "Information systems outsourcing: A survey and analysis of the literature", *The DATA BASE for Advances in Infomation Systems*, 35 (4): 6-102.

Dibbern, J.; Winkler, J.; Heinzl, A. (2008), "Explaining variations in client extra costs between software projects offshored to India", *MIS Quarterly*, 32 (2): 333-366.

Erber, G.; Sayed-Ahmed, A. (2008), "Offshore outsourcing: A global shift in the present IT industry", *Intereconomics*, 40 (2): 100–112.

Gefen, D.; Wyss, S.; Lichtenstein, Y. (2008), "Business familiarity as risk mitigation in software development outsourcing contracts", *MIS Quarterly*, 32 (3): 531-551.

Gsell, B.; Overhage, S.; Turowski, K. (2008), "Unzureichende Leistungsbeschreibung bei der Softwareentwicklung und die Rolle von Standardverträgen", in Möllers, T. (ed.), *Standardisierung durch Markt und Recht*, Nomos, Baden-Baden: 23-48.

Hall, A. (1990), "Seven myths of formal methods", *IEEE Software*, 7 (5): 11-19.

Hansen, H.; Neumann, G. (2009), *Wirtschaftsinformatik 1: Grundlagen und Anwendung*, 10th edn, Lucius & Lucius, Stuttgart.

Heeks, R.; Krishna, S.; Nicholson, B.; Sahay, S. (2001), "Synching or sinking: Global software outsourcing relationships", *IEEE Software*, 18 (2): 54-60.

Heindl, M.; Biffl, S. (2006), "Risk management with enhanced tracing of requirements rationale in highly distributed projects", *Proceedings of the 2006 international workshop on global software development for the practitioner*, ACM, Shanghai, China: 20–26.

Hevner, A.; March, S.; Park, J.; Ram, S. (2004), "Design science in information systems research", *MIS Quarterly*, 28 (1): 75–105.

Hofstede, G. (2002), *Culture's consequences: Comparing values, behaviors, institutions, and organizations across nations*, 2nd edn, Sage, Thousand Oaks, USA.

IEEE (1998), *IEEE recommended practice for software requirements specifications: IEEE standard 830-1998*, IEEE, New York, USA.

King, W.; Torkzadeh, G. (2008), "Information systems offshoring: Research status and issues", *MIS Quarterly*, 32 (2): 205-225.

Klein, R.; Scholl, A. (2004), *Planung und Entscheidung: Konzepte, Modelle und Methoden einer modernen betriebswirtschaftlichen Entscheidungsanalyse*, Vahlen, Munich.

Kobitzsch, W.; Rombach, D.; Feldmann, R. (2001), "Outsourcing in India", *IEEE Software*, 18 (2): 78-86.

Kojima, S.; Kojima, M. (2007), "Making IT offshoring work for the Japanese industries", *Proceedings of the first international conference on software engineering approaches for offshore and outsourced development*, Lecture Notes in Computer Science 4716, Springer, 5-7 Feb. 2007, Zurich, Switzerland: 67-82.

Krogstie, J. (1998), "Integrating the understanding of quality in requirements specifications and conceptual modeling", *ACM SIGSOFT Software Engineering Notes*, 23 (1): 86-91.

van Lamsweerde, A. (2009), *Requirements engineering: From system goals to UML models to software specifications*, Wiley, Hoboken, USA.

Liskov, B.; Berzins, V. (1986), "An appraisal of program specifications", in Gehani, N.; McGettrick, A. (eds), *Software specification techniques*, Addison Wesley, Wokingham, UK: 3-24.

MacGregor, E.; Hsieh, Y.; Kruchten, P. (2005), "Cultural patterns in software process mishaps: Incidents in global projects", *ACM SIGSOFT Software Engineering Notes*, 30 (4): 1-5.

Moczadlo, R. (2002), "Chancen und Risiken des Offshore-Development: Empirische Analyse der Erfahrunge deutscher Unternehmen", accessed on 14 Jul. 2009, http://www.competence-site.de.

Morris, C. (1970), *Foundation of the theory of signs*, University of Chicago Press, Chicago, USA.

Nevo, S.; Wade, M.; Cook, W. (2006), "An examination of the trade-off between internal and external IT capabilities", *Journal of Strategic Information Systems*, 16 (1): 5-23.

Overby, S. (2003), "Offshore outsourcing the money: Moving jobs overseas can be a much more expensive proposition than you may think", *CIO*, 16 (22): 60-66.

Overhage, S. (2006), "Vereinheitlichte Spezifikation von Komponenten: Grundlagen, UnSCom Spezifikationsrahmen und Anwendung", Dissertation, Universität Augsburg, Augsburg.

Overhage, S.; Thomas, P. (2005), "WS-Specification: Ein Spezifikationsrahmen zur Beschreibung von Web-Services auf Basis des UDDI-Standards", *eEconomy, eGovernment, eSociety: Proceedings Wirtschaftsinformatik 2005*, Physica, 23-25 Feb. 2005, Bamberg: 1539-1558.

Pruß, M.; Skroch, O. (2008), "Kritische Defizite bei der Leistungsvereinbarung in Softwareverträgen: Ein Bericht aus der Praxis", in Möllers, T. (ed.), *Vielfalt und Einheit: Wirtschaftliche und rechtliche Rahmenbedingungen von Standardbildung*, Nomos, Baden-Baden: 263-278.

Pryor, B.; Keane, B. (2004), "Critical success factors in outsourcing", *Offshore oursourcing - risks and rewards: Symposium conclusions paper*, CFO Publishing, 17 Jun. 2004, New York, USA: 11-13.

Remus, U.; Wiener, M. (2009), "Critical success factors for managing offshore software development projects", *Journal of Global Information Technology Management*, 12 (1): 6-29.

Sakthivel, S. (2007), "Managing risk in offshore systems development", *Communications of the ACM*, 50 (4): 69-75.

Scheffczyk, J.; Stutz, C.; Borghoff, U.; Siedersleben, J. (2004), "Formale Konsistenzsicherung in informellen Software-Spezifikationen", *Informatik Forschung und Entwicklung*, 19 (1): 17-29.

Schienmann, B. (1997), *Objektorientierter Fachentwurf: Ein terminologiebasierter Ansatz für die Konstruktion von Anwendungssystemen*, Teubner, Stuttgart.

Setamanit, S.; Raffo, D. (2008), "Identifying key success factors for globally distributed software projects using simulation: A case study", *Proceedings of the international conference on software processes*, Lecture Notes in Computer Science 5007, Springer, 10-11 May 2008, Leipzig: 320-332.

Siakas, K.; Maoutsidis, D.; Siakas, E. (2006), "Trust facilitating good software outsourcing relationships", *Proceedings of the 13th European conference on software process improvement*, Lecture Notes in Computer Science 4257, Springer, 11-13 Oct 2006, Joensuu, Finland: 171-182.

Steimle, T. (2007), *Softwareentwicklung im Offshoring: Erfolgsfaktoren für die Praxis*, Springer, Heidelberg.

Takeda, H.; Veerkamp, P.; Tomiyama, T.; Yoshikawa, H. (2007), "Modeling design processes", *AI Magazine*, 11 (4): 37-48.

Tsuji, H.; Sakurai, A.; Yoshida, K.; Tiwana, A.; Bush, A. (2007), "Questionnaire-based risk assessment scheme for Japanese offshore software outsourcing", *Proceedings of the first international conference on software engineering approaches for offshore and outsourced development*, Lecture Notes in Computer Science 4716, Springer, 5-7 Feb. 2007, Zurich, Switzerland: 114-127.

Vlaar, P.; van Fenema, P.; Tiwari, V. (2008), "Cocreating understanding and value in distributed work: How members of onsite and offshore vendor teams give, make, demand and break sense", *MIS Quarterly*, 32 (2): 227-255.

Wada, Y.; Nakahigashi, D.; Tsuji, H. (2007), "An evaluation method for offshore software development by structural equation modeling", *Proceedings of the first international conference on software engineering approaches for offshore and outsourced development*, Lecture Notes in Computer Science 4716, Springer, 5-7 Feb. 2007, Zurich, Switzerland: 128-140.

Wehrmann, A.; Gull, D. (2006), "Ein COCOMO-basierter Ansatz zur Entscheidungsunterstützung beim Offshoring von Softwareentwicklungsprojekten", *Wirtschaftsinformatik*, 48 (6): 407-417.

Winkler, J.; Dibbern, J.; Heinzl, A. (2007), "Der Einfluß kultureller Unterschiede beim IT-Offshoring: Ergebnisse aus Fallstudien zu deutsch-indischen Anwendungsentwickungsprojekten", *Wirtschaftsinformatik*, 49 (2): 95-103.

Zangemeister, C. (1976), *Nutzwertanalyse in der Systemtechnik – Eine Methodik zur multidimensionalen Bewertung und Auswahl von Projektalternativen*, 4th edn, Wittemann, Munich.

IV   Selection

IV.R5   Optimal stopping for the run-time self-adaptation of software systems [5]

Advanced software systems can reconfigure themselves at run-time by choosing between alternative options for performing certain functions. Such options can be built into the systems, but are also externally available on open and uncontrolled platforms. Main examples are Web services and mashups on the Internet today.

The following research article shows how run-time software self-adaptation with uncontrolled external options can be optimized by stopping theory, yielding the best possible lower probability bound for choosing an optimal option. The article presents two application scenarios and derives the respective, efficient optimization algorithms. The theory is confirmed by simulating examples for both scenarios where the improvement over an assumed closed software system is measured.

[5] Research article R5: Skroch, O.; Turowski, K. (2010), "Optimal stopping for the run-time self-adaptation of software systems", *Journal of Information & Optimization Sciences*, 31 (1): 147–157.
© TARU Publications, New Delhi, India for the original contribution.

1   Introduction

Flexible software systems are based on the concept of modularity. They can be constructed through component-based and service-oriented software engineering approaches. These approaches promote the reuse of software that has already been made available before. Ideally, a larger application can be build by identifying already existing, suitable components or services first, and then composing the parts into a loosely coupled, larger system. The resulting larger software system jointly performs all operations required, while mutual dependencies between its parts are fully explicit (Achermann & Nierstrasz 2005; Parnas 1972; Szyperski, Grunz & Murer 2002).

Selecting suitable components and services is one decisive step in composing such software systems. In component-based and service-oriented approaches, suitable components and services can be identified by searching through software repositories or electronic markets. It can be done at build-time when designing and implementing the application. This leads to a closed software architecture where all components and services are internal parts of the larger system. Closed systems can already provide internal run-time self-adaptation capabilities. One example are VoIP *(Voice over Internet Protocol)* clients which can select, from a number of codec options integrated at build-time, one suitable codec according to actual data rates measured at run-time.

Advanced software architectures can perform parts of their functionality also through external components or services that were not integrated into the software. Such external components or services could be unknown at build-time, but on open and uncontrolled software platforms they may become available in large numbers later at run-time. Prominent examples on the Internet are Web services in general (Atkinson et al. 2002) and service mashups in particular (Bernstein & Haas 2008; Gamble & Gamble 2008).

Exhaustive run-time search for better service options is impossible on huge open platforms such as the Internet. Anonymous, independent services from distributed open platforms are unknown and can not be controlled either. At first glance, searching under these conditions seemingly can be improved with heuristics only. Still we propose an exact algorithmic optimization for self-adaptation processes under these conditions: to determine the best moment when to stop a search for further service options. From stopping theory, we derive and simulate efficient algorithms that implement a search strategy with the best possible lower probability bound for choosing an optimal self-adaptation option.

The rest of the paper is structured as follows. Chapter 2 explains the required background and states assumptions made. Chapter 3 lines out two different run-time self-adaptation scenarios and presents the applicable stopping theory for both scenarios. Chapter 4 applies the theory to both scenarios, derives actual algorithms, and presents results from two extended simulation examples, where advantages over a corresponding static software system are measured. Chapter 5 summarizes and concludes the paper.

2   Flexible software architectures and matching schemes for self-adaptation

Figure IV.R5-1 illustrates in an example how services are supplied and requested through service interfaces in component software system architectures. The two decisive principles are composition and delegation. A requested service interface can be composed with a supplied service interface, to combine into aggregated components. Service interfaces can be delegated to other service interfaces of the same type, to hand over processing. Supplied service interfaces are available from other components or even from open platforms.

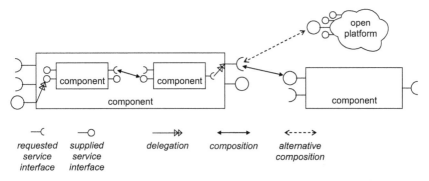

Figure IV.R5-1: Component software architecture example. Based on Shaw and Garlan (1996).

Composition implies to match supplied interfaces with requested interfaces. Figure IV.R5-2 suggests a classification of the possible schemes for matching supplied service options in existing compositions. The set of n supplied service options from external, uncontrolled platforms can be large. The set of m compositions from within the closed software can also be large, but $n \gg m$.

- The choice scheme compares one composition – a requested service with its supplied service – against the alternative composition of this same requested service with one different supplied service option. It is the elementary decision whether the present composition or the alternative composition is better. This scheme is also the basic consideration for the other schemes.

- The allocation scheme checks one particular service option for many or all compositions. Allocation can be seen as a repetition of choice, trying one supplied option in all compositions.

- The search scheme checks many supplied service options for one particular composition. Search can be seen as a repetition of choice, trying one composition with all supplied options.

- The screening scheme checks many or all compositions with many supplied service options each. Screening is the most general approach and can be seen as allocation with search.

$n \gg m$	Open Platform n external options	
Closed System m internal compositions	**Choice** 1 composition : 1 option	**Search** 1 composition : n options
	Allocation m compositions : 1 option	**Screening** m compositions : n options

Figure IV.R5-2: Possible matching schemes.

Run-time software self-adaptation aims at dynamically re-composing services. Service options supplied at run-time via open platforms are assumed to fit function wise, but may differ in other ways such as quality, cost, etc. For a given composition it is possible to improve such non-functional system features by selecting a best supplied service option and by adapting the system accordingly (it can be assumed that the set of supplied options is never empty, if we consider the internal service supply as fallback if no external option is chosen).

Run-time software self-adaptation is triggered by the adapting system itself. Before a requested service interface calls the supplied interface at run-time, the system looks for externally supplied options and decides whether to re-compose this service call. This implies matching operations from the search scheme and excludes the allocation scheme. It can be assumed that the utility function is to choose the best available option, and that the actual values for the comparison can be determined by the system. The related computing can be done, for example, in an adaptation component that orchestrates and monitors the re-compositions.

Independent services from open software platforms cannot be controlled. One consequence is that any supplied service can be unavailable or changed in the next moment. This implies that the final decision whether to choose a certain service must be made straightforward. Consequently, for the search scheme it is not possible to memorize a supplied service option and, after further unsuccessful search, get back and use this service option.

Software self-adaptation can be performance critical. With n and m both large and $n \gg m$, the screening scheme is not feasible for run-time matching operations (screening is relevant at build-time rather). But even the search scheme on open platforms already requires efficient calculation methods with a large number of available service options n.

3   Optimal stopping in two self-adaptation scenarios

We examine two simple scenarios that avoid exhaustive search and generally enable the application of run-time self-adaptation with uncontrolled external options in the described situation. Firstly, either one limits the number of options to be considered from the many available options. Or, secondly, one allows only a maximum run-time delay. Stopping theory can be used in both scenarios to optimize the run-time software self-adaptation process by determining the best point to stop the search for further alternative options.

Stopping problems are a well known research topic in mathematical statistics. A general solution approach to our problem class can be found already in (Lindley 1961) and within the framework of stopping Markov chains in (Dynkin & Juschkewitsch 1969). Common strategies for optimal stopping under considerations suitable for the two scenarios are described in (Bruss 1984) and (Bruss 2000).

3.1   Limited number of run-time options

The first scenario limits the number of alternative options n which can be considered for self-adaptation. This means that the self-adaptation process evaluates supplied service options at most up to this limited number, and the limit is predefined.

With a predefined, limited number of unknown and independent options, let $I_1, I_2, \ldots, I_n \in \{0; 1\}$ be independent indicator functions defined on a probability space (Ω, A, P). An index k is called a success if $I_k = 1$. The indicators are observed in sequence $I_1, I_2, \ldots$ It is possible to stop at any of them but it is not possible to recall any preceding.

Let T be the class of stopping rules τ so that $\{\tau = k\} \in \sigma(I_1, I_2, \ldots, I_k)$ which represents the sigma-algebra generated by the indicator sequence. The optimal stopping rule $\tau^* \in$ T maximizes the probability of the event $I_\tau = 1$ and $I_{\tau+1} = I_{\tau+2} = \ldots = I_n = 0$.

Now let $p_j = E(I_j)$ be the probabilities for the independent indicators. Let $q_j := 1 - p_j$ and the so-called odds $r_j := p_j / q_j$. The optimal rule τ^* for stopping on the last success is to stop on the first index (if any) k with $I_k = 1$ and $k \geq s$ where

$$s = \sup\left\{1, \sup\left\{1 \le k \le n : \sum_{j=k}^{n} r_j \ge 1\right\}\right\} \quad \text{with } \sup\{\varnothing\} := -\infty \qquad \text{(IV.R5-1)}$$

Rule (IV.R5-1) is intuitive. The optimal strategy is to add up the odds $r_n + r_{n-1} + \dots$ ("backwards") until this sum becomes equal to or greater than one, at index s, and then to stop at the first index $k \ge s$ with a success. In other words, it is optimal to stop as soon as the expected number of future successes becomes equal to or less than one. Then, the value (probability for the best choice) is $1/e$, given by

$$V(n) = \prod_{j=s}^{n} q_j \sum_{j=s}^{n} r_j = Q_s(n) R_s(n) \qquad \text{(IV.R5-2)}$$

This is the odds theorem of optimal stopping, proven in (Bruss 2000).

3.2   Limited run-time delay

The second scenario defines a maximum length for the time frame that can be used for a self-adaptation call at run-time, while the number of supplied service options is not known or cannot reasonably be predefined (except that it is known that there are many options).

Then, with a distribution function $F(z)$ on the real time interval $[0; t_{max}]$, let $Z_1, Z_2, \dots$ be independent random variables (each with a continuous distribution function F) where Z_k is the arrival time of option k. Let N be a non-negative integer random variable independent of all Z_k so that N represents the unknown total number of supplied options. With $N = n$, each arrival order $\langle 1 \rangle, \langle 2 \rangle, \dots, \langle n \rangle$ is equally likely. Since the best service option needs to be selected, it only makes sense to accept an option that is better than all previous ones, and all previous ones must have been evaluated.

The waiting time x is defined as the time up to which all options are evaluated without accepting, while the value of the leading option is remembered. The first leading option after time x is accepted, if there is one, and all options are refused, if there is none. This is called the x-strategy.

For any distribution with $P(N > 0) > 0$ there exists a waiting time x^* maximizing the success probability for the x-strategy. Moreover, for all $\varepsilon > 0$ there is an integer m where $n \ge m$ implies

$$x^* \in \left[\frac{1}{e_F} - \varepsilon; \frac{1}{e_F}\right] \quad \text{where} \quad \frac{1}{e_F} = \inf\left\{x \mid F(x) = \frac{1}{e}\right\} \qquad \text{(IV.B5-3)}$$

Rule (IV.R5-3) is the only waiting time policy with the asymptotically best possible success probability $\geq 1/e$, regardless of the distribution of N. This is the $1/e$ law of optimal stopping, proven in (Bruss 1984).

4   Application and simulation

Optimal stopping can be applied to optimize the run-time self-adaptation of software systems searching for options on open platforms. No literature was found describing this application, except for the authors' previous research (Skroch & Turowski 2007).

4.1   Limited number of run-time options

The odds theorem (Bruss 2000) can be applied to optimize the first scenario of run-time software self-adaptation. Let the best alternative option show up at j and let the stopping index be s. The best service option will therefore be selected only if $j > s$, and only if the "second best" service option before j appears at i with $i \leq s$, which happens in s out of j-1 cases. Each permutation of the trial sequence is equally likely. So the probability for the best service option at position j is $1/n$ and the probability for the second best service option among the first s is $s/(j-1)$. The probability P_n that the best service option is selected summarizes (over all $j = s+1, s+2, \ldots, n$) the probability for the best service option at position j times the probability for the "second best" service option among the first s:

$$P_s = \sum_{j=s+1}^{n} \left(\frac{1}{n} \frac{s}{j-1} \right) = \frac{s}{n} \sum_{j=s}^{n-1} \frac{1}{j} \tag{IV.R5-4}$$

(IV.R5-4) yields $R_s = 1/(n-1) + 1/(n-2) + \ldots$ stopped at $R_s = 1$. At the optimum, i.e. the stopping index s, as $n \to \infty$ it can be recognized that $s/n \to 1/e$ and also $V_s(n) \to 1/e$. The value $1/e$ (≈ 0.368) is a typical lower bound well-known from the classical best choice problem. See also Lindley (1961), Bruss (2000).

The implemented algorithm therefore matches service options with the internal composition and rejects all options, while memorizing the value of the best option yet. After a proportion of n/e of the options has passed, the next leading option is chosen, if there is one. Otherwise no alternative choice is made and the original composition remains in place. Since n is predefined in this first scenario, n/e is a constant.

The algorithm is efficient. Additional time complexity is $O(n)$ in the worst case, linear on the number of evaluated options, because for each evaluated option, one single comparison is made against the previously best option. In the best case a leading option appears immediately after n/e, adding constant complexity only. Additional space complexity is constant even in the worst case, because at any time only one value (the best yet) is stored.

For this first "limited options" scenario, an example was simulated with Web services offering currency exchange rates of different age. It can be assumed that more recent exchange rates are better.

Exp.	Avg. quality	Best was selected
1	879.3	0.29
2	879.3	0.33
3	894.5	0.38
4	906.3	0.29
5	867.6	0.32
Avg.	885.4	0.32

Table IV.R5-1: Results from simulation experiments for the "limited options" scenario.

In the simulation experiments, uniformly distributed quality values between 0 (worst) and 999 (best) were randomly assigned to the compositions with external service options. The internal composition was given an assumed fixed value of 700. These assumptions simplify the simulation without loss of generality as to our intended experimental demonstration. The proposed optimization method does not require any particular quality measurement function, except that it has to produce at least ordinal results for the matching operation.

Five experiments with 100 self-adaptations in each run were simulated. The limit n was set to 1000 service options. Table IV.R5-1 shows results from the first simulation.

With a predefined number of evaluated options, the run-time self-adaptation example with optimal stopping outperformed the assumed closed software system by 167.6 to 206.3 quality points. The average improvement was 185.4 points, or 26.5 percent, over all five "limited options" experiments together. The best available service was actually selected in 32 percent of the self-adaptation trials (where the theoretical prediction is 36.8 percent).

4.2   Limited run-time delay

The $1/e$ law (Bruss 1984) can be applied to optimize the second scenario of run-time software self-adaptation. With many suitable service options available on open platforms, a uniform distribution over time is assumed for service discovery.

Take $x = F(z)$, $z \in [0; t_{max}]$ with a continuous time scale x between 0 and 1 and with each $X_k = F(Z_k)$ uniform on $[0; 1]$. A stopped search ends optimal if the best service option $\langle 1 \rangle$

arrives in $]x;1]$ before all other service options arriving in $]x;1]$ which are better than the best of those which arrived in $]0; x]$. From the $k+1$ best options the option $\langle k+1 \rangle$ arrives in $]0; x]$ and the k best ones in $]x;1]$ with probability $x(1-x)^k$. Since $\langle 1 \rangle$ arrives before $\langle 2 \rangle,...,\langle k \rangle$ with probability $1/k$ one obtains the success probability:

$$P_n(x) = x\sum_{k=1}^{n}\frac{1}{k}(1-x)^k = x\sum_{k=1}^{n-1}\frac{1}{k}(1-x)^k + \frac{1}{n}(1-x)^n \quad \text{with } n \geq 2 \qquad \text{(IV.R5-5)}$$

The sum term of (IV.R5-5) contains the Taylor expansion of $-\ln(x)$. As $n \to \infty$ one obtains $P_n(x) \to -x\ln(x)$ which has a unique maximum at $x = 1/e$. The value $1/e$ (≈ 0.368) is the (asymptotically) best possible lower bound. See also Lindley (1961), Bruss (1984).

The respective algorithm therefore matches service options with the internal composition and rejects all options, while memorizing the value of the best option yet. With a uniform distribution of service discovery events, as soon as a proportion of t/e of the predefined time frame has passed the next leading service option is chosen, if there is one. Otherwise no alternative choice is made and the original composition remains in place. Since t is predefined in this second scenario, t/e is a constant.

The algorithm is again efficient. Additional time complexity is constant even in the worst case, because the maximum length of the time frame t is preset. Additional space complexity is also constant even in the worst case, because at any time only one value (the best yet) is stored.

For this second "limited delay" scenario, simulation examples were conducted with settings according to the "limited options" case. In the "limited delay" simulation five experiments were conducted with 500 self-adaptations each, 1000 supplied service options were available for each self-adaptation, and the maximum run-time delay t was set to 200 milliseconds. Table IV.R5-2 shows results from the second simulation.

Exp.	Avg. quality	Best was selected
1	874.0	0.376
2	877.2	0.364
3	870.3	0.354
4	856.7	0.294
5	872.0	0.350
Avg.	870.0	0.348

Table IV.R5-2: Results from simulation experiments for the "limited delay" scenario.

On a predefined maximum delay of the matching operation, the run-time self-adaptation example with optimal stopping performed 156.7 to 177.2 quality points better than the assumed closed software system. The average improvement was 170.0 points, or 24.3 percent, over all five "limited delay" runs together. The best available service was actually selected in 34,8 percent of the service calls (where the theoretical prediction is 36.8 percent).

5   Summary and conclusion

Stopping theory has been used to optimize the run-time self-adaptation of advanced, dynamic software systems in two scenarios. One scenario predefined the maximum number of options at run-time. The other scenario predefined the maximum run-time delay. For both scenarios, suitable stopping theory was applied and efficient algorithms were derived. Simulation experiments showed that dynamic software systems with run-time self-adaptation and optimal stopping outperform a corresponding static software system.

A major driver for the applicability of the results is the increasing use of open platforms for distributed, service-oriented systems and mashups. Important application areas already include grid computing, distributed multimedia, mobile computing, and self-healing software. With few changes, the results are applicable also for the run-time self-adaptation of software systems to dynamically changing requirements.

References

Achermann, F.; Nierstrasz, O. (2005), "A calculus for reasoning about software composition", *Theoretical Computer Science*, 331 (2-3): 367-396.

Atkinson, C.; Bunse, C.; Groß, H.; Kühne, T. (2002), "Towards a general component model for Web-based applications", *Annals of Software Engineering*, 13 (1): 35-69.

Bernstein, P.; Haas, L. (2008), "Information integration in the enterprise", *Communications of the ACM*, 51 (9): 72-79.

Bruss, T. (1984), "A unified approach to a class of best choice problems with an unknown number of options", *The Annals of Probability*, 12 (3): 882-889.

Bruss, T. (2000), "Sum the odds to one and stop", *The Annals of Probability*, 28 (3): 1384-1391.

Dynkin, E.; Juschkewitsch, A. (1969), *Sätze und Aufgaben über Markoffsche Prozesse*, Springer, Heidelberg.

Gamble, T.; Gamble, R. (2008), "Monoliths to mashups: Increasing opportunistic assets", *IEEE Software*, 25 (6): 71-79.

Lindley, D. (1961), "Dynamic programming and decision theory", *Applied Statistics*, 10 (1): 39-51.

Parnas, D. (1972), "On the criteria to be used in decomposing systems into modules", *Communications of the ACM*, 15 (12): 1053-1058.

Shaw, M.; Garlan, D. (1996), *Software architecture: Perspectives on an emerging discipline*, Prentice Hall, Upper Saddle River, USA.

Skroch, O.; Turowski, K. (2007), "Improving service selection in component-based architectures with optimal stopping", *Proceedings of the 34th Euromicro conference on software engineering and advanced applications*, IEEE Computer Society, 28-31 Aug. 2007, Lübeck: 39-46.

Szyperski, C.; Gruntz, D.; Murer, S. (2002), *Component software: Beyond object-oriented programming*, 2nd edn, Addison Wesley, London, UK.

IV.R6   Reducing domain level scenarios to test component-based software [6]

Higher-order black box software tests can be used for checking independent end-user domain requirements. This has become an issue of increasing importance with compositional reuse of software artifacts. The following research article elaborates on a method for deriving testable scenarios directly from a customer domain model by abstraction, reduction, and inclusion for critical coverage. The resulting linear (i.e., non-branching) scenarios can be extended to serve as references or oracles for testing the specifications of components and services offered by suppliers.

The article presents the proposed method in an overview and elaborates on the domain reduction step within the process for the generation of testable scenarios from a domain model. An example is provided which is non-fictitious on the domain side. Advantages of the method are an underlying clear business model, test oracles that are independent from the software development process, and validation results that can be generated early in the development cycle, possibly before the software itself is available.

---

[6] Research article R6: Skroch, O.; Turowski, K. (2007), "Reducing domain level scenarios to test component-based software", *Journal of Software*, 2 (5): 64-73.
© Academy Publisher, Oulu, Finland for the original contribution.

1   Introduction

Software engineering is in the process of evolving from a craft to an industry and reuse is one decisive element that supports and propels this evolution. Reuse has even been described as "the only realistic approach" (Mili, Mili & Mili 1995, p. 529) to meet the needs of a software industry. Recently, further increasing needs for reuse have been listed among the top trends that will influence future software processes (Boehm 2005).

Compositional reuse is one of the fundamental software reuse technologies (Biggerstaff & Richter 1987). The approach is to reuse executable artifacts which are found in repositories, and compose them into larger applications (Szyperski, Gruntz & Murer 2002). Compositional reuse of black box business components is part of the overall concept of component-based business applications, where business components are described by multi-layered and semi-formal specifications, implement services from a business domain, and are envisaged to be traded on markets (Turowski 2003). Such compositional reuse includes

- building software for reuse, by creating self contained, marketable, fully described black box artifacts on the supply side,

- building software from reuse, by composing larger applications from these executable stand-alone artifacts on the demand side, and

- trading the associated software artifacts or components on a market (possibly an internal market within a corporation).

In this environment, the demand side – customers and end-users of component software – looks for useful software components and does not want to access source code but restricts to a black box view. The demand side focus therefore is on "higher-order" (Myers 1979, pp. 103ff) compliance of domain level pragmatics and semantics, while mere formal and syntactical compliance is often perceived as technical precondition in the responsibility of the supply side.

Software component reuse with parts that can be looked up in catalogues and can then be integrated into large applications similar to electronic parts has been proposed already since long (McIlroy 1968). But non-trivial problems still complicate broad compositional software reuse in theory and in practice today. Among the problems on the demand side is the evaluation of available components against their more complex end-user domain requirements: assuming that an offered component complies syntactically, it still needs to be tested if its pragmatics and semantics are useful for a specific domain automation purpose.

In traditional engineering disciplines, the importance of testing is well acknowledged because of a long history of experiences. In software engineering it is on the one hand known that software is fundamentally less reliable than traditional engineering products (Parnas 2001) and that building software will probably always be hard (Brooks 1987). On the other hand the well-known notion of "good-enough software" (Yourdon 1995, p. 79) shows that we have to deal with a pragmatic view on quality aspects of software, in particular with large enterprise applications.

But also good enough software development can profit from testing, especially with enterprise-sized systems if errors are found efficiently and early in the development process. Firstly, it was shown that the effort for error correction grows markedly when the error is detected later. Secondly, the earlier errors are detected the more rectification alternatives are available. Thirdly, studies in science and projects in industry indicate that testing takes more than fifty percent of the effort even with non-safety critical software.

Software testing is even more important whenever prefabricated items such as components are reused. Firstly, a single component made for reuse must be more thoroughly tested than a component made to be used once because it is reused in combinations unknown at the time of development. Secondly, a system based on a configuration of multiple black box components from different suppliers must be more thoroughly tested as compared to large pre-integrated products. Cf. (Meyer 2003).

The distinction between technology based supplier testing and domain based customer testing is widely acknowledged, in particular with component-based software (Weyuker 1998; Gao, Tsao & Wu 2003). Recently, an approach was proposed specifically for component validation testing on the domain level of the demand side (Skroch 2007). It is based on testable scenarios which are independently derived from an end-user domain and become checked against reuse specifications from suppliers.

The rest of the paper presents and elaborates the method and is structured as follows. Section two of the paper sets out basic assumptions and presents the underlying business model. Section three introduces the approach in an overview, elaborates on the process reduction through an abstracted business domain, and finally applies the method in a small example, non-fictitious on the domain side. Section four elaborates on the current state of the art and on existing solutions, and delimits the contributions of the method. Section five summarizes and concludes this paper.

2 Basic assumptions and business model

Dynamics and pragmatism of real life businesses demand good enough software which is useful to the customer, and therefore support a focus on higher-order domain tests. So our approach is based on the fundamental assumption that the final arbiter of software success is only the customer to whom the component software is useful or not. This most central assumption was stated already in 1979: "*A software error is present when the program does not do what its end user reasonably expects it to do.*" (Myers 1979, p. 103).

The end-user domain is the area of intended application for the component-based software. While it usually lacks a fully formal definition or model, we still assume that customer test references from the application domain prevail over test oracles created with mere supplier knowledge from within the component software technology. Higher-order testing on the domain level, without the intention to change or reengineer components or their specifications, initially has as a goal to validate the suppliers' software for reuse and control on the demand side. The argument of assertive and independent consideration of the ontological domain and the supporting technologies can be founded in Ψ (psi) theory (Dietz 2006).

From an end-user's domain point of view, it is favorable to test higher-order requirements independently and as early as possible. This supports the identification and assessment of components, if possible at best before the executable software itself is available. The necessary validation knowledge consists of testable business requirements that predefine what the right software solution is supposed to do, and it needs to be constructed.

Our construction approach is embedded into a clear business model assumption derived from the vision of industrialized compositional reuse for software engineering, which has been described in detail in (Turowski 2003). Figure IV.R6-1, notation "e3-value" (Gordijn & Akkermans 2001), introduces the underlying business model assumption with the three actors: component supply, component demand and component market.

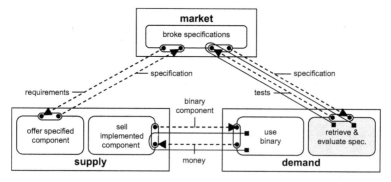

Figure IV.R6-1: Business model assumption.

In the business model, suppliers create components for an anonymous market to satisfy an assumed demand or requirement on that market. These requirements can typically be acquired from discussions with individual clients but also could very well be entrepreneurial market assumptions. Software components offered to cover the requirements are technically mature and suppliers keep their source code undisclosed. They completely specify their components in black box style by fully defining the interfaces to convey the components' contracts (what the components do) but without disclosing their implementation details (how the components work) (Meyer 1992). Specifications achieving this are multi-layered and semi-formal today. Respective specification approaches are proposed e.g. in (Overhage 2006; Ackermann et al. 2002) where contract levels and facts to be specified describe the external view onto the component for reuse. These component specifications can serve as black box description for reuse and are put into publicly available component specification libraries.

Component software users on the demand side want support and automation for their requirements and search a wide variety of library components for the right software. The available components are found as specifications e.g. on the Internet. These semi-formal, multi-layered component reuse specifications represent the candidates offered by suppliers for domain testing. Customers query the black box functional specifications with specific predefined criteria, retrieve matches, and then evaluate the retrieved specifications in detail. Both retrieval and evaluation imply a comparison i.e. a test between reference features demanded and specification candidates offered.

Compositional reuse acknowledges the industrial segregation between a supply side offering components for reuse and a demand side requiring software built from reused and properly orchestrated parts. Such industry-style compositional reuse apparently requires advances to established software engineering methods, which also includes the testing stage. An important challenge for black box reuse at this point is how to derive reasonable specification retrieval and evaluation criteria, and that means: how to validate testable end-user domain requirements against supplier specifications.

The associated testing may be classified as specification based or program based, and specification based testing can be divided into state based testing and black box testing (Vincenzi et al. 2003). The component paradigm of the described business model assumes that components are tested on the basis of their specifications, and restrict our approach to black box testing. It is acknowledged that good overall testing will be comprehensive and will employ a set of complementary methods in practice. It is also acknowledged that testing alone can not improve the quality of software, but early and expressive test results can improve decisions.

3   Constructing linear scenarios

3.1   ARIval overview

A precondition for the validation of requirements is that these requirements are stated in testable terms. Figure IV.R6-2, notation "activity diagram" (Object Management Group 2005), gives an overview on the ARIval (abstraction, reduction, inclusion, validation) method (Skroch 2007), where domain level scenarios are used to validate aspects of multi-layered component reuse specifications, if possible showing that the specified software works for the higher-order domain requirements.

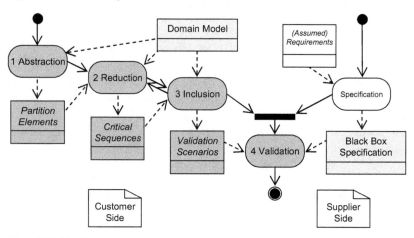

Figure IV.R6-2: ARIval overview.

To construct testable business requirements on the customer side, our first starting point is the observation that also for testing higher-order domain functionality, only a small subset of the full domain is actually relevant for the end-users' intended automation with distinct effects on utilized system behavior.

The second starting point is the observation that some kind of domain model is usually available on the customer side, in many cases through prosaic business rules and process descriptions as semi formal or informal models, e.g. activity diagram, event-driven process chain, Petri net, etc. Full or partial automation is required for the model, or parts of it, from ready-made software components.

Relevant parts of the model environment are first abstracted based on the well-known equivalence partitioning and boundary value analysis, which is described and used for program testing since the late 1970s (Myers 1979). This results in domain partition elements which are a discrete representation of the original continuous domain, with one representative element per partition.

The abstracted elements are then reduced, by identifying reasonable and critical sequences. Complexity of typical requirements in real settings will lead to very many possible sequences at this point and prevent an exhaustive testing. This means that with each possible sequence of steps that requires automation on the domain side, and with the corresponding sequence of equivalence classes, a small number of critical sequences need to be selected from the very large number of all possibilities.

Selection criteria are domain centric and come from outside of the software engineering process. They include domain workflow and value flow considerations e.g. on frequency, criticality, financial or other risk, external visibility, etc. instead of software centric objectives such as coverage of all control statements in the source code. Furthermore, the sequences must not contain branching but make up linear paths in order to avoid quantitative evaluation problems during actual testing (cf. state explosion). To achieve this, a critical sequence with branches becomes de-branched until we have a number of linear sequences instead.

The abstracted and reduced domain part then contains value representatives in sequences, with each sequence linear and deemed critical by the customer for the intended application.

An inclusion will use the critical linear sequences to build scenarios, both within a domain part and across a number of different related domain parts, to cover the critical paths in their context as full business transaction flows. These scenarios must again not contain branching but make up linear paths. This can be guaranteed by constructing them accordingly, i.e. instead of a branching scenario we include two or more branch-free scenarios, until all resulting scenarios are linear at the end.

The method provides the possibility to re-iterate the reduction step, e.g. if certain sequences are found missing one can go back and establish them to be available for the construction of the respective end-to-end scenario. In this way each linear scenario is deliberately and consciously included into the validation step, or not. Inclusion criteria, again, are domain centric and are derived from considerations rooting in domain ontology instead of software technology, as described.

Finally, the actual testing will numerically check applicable parts of the reuse specifications from the supply side using all formally defined and branch-free critical validation scenarios as test cases.

Three basic coverage measures can be defined. Two start from the abstracted domain, which is an equivalent of the original domain. Reduction coverage measures the abstracted domain against reduced sequences requirements. Inclusion coverage measures reduced sequences against included scenarios. The third measure starts from the set of scenarios. Validation coverage measures a scenario's expected results against the actual validation success. The measures could be plain and weighted. The weighted coverage would scale on numeric scores given for each reduction criteria, inclusion criteria and scenario, e.g. by using a simple ranking.

Beneficiaries of the method are mainly customers and end-users in the presented business model. The ARIVal method supports them in evaluating the many component specifications from repositories on the basis of their testable requirements, independently derived from their ontological domain, and before actual software is available.

3.2   Process flow transformation and blocking

Through data abstraction, based on equivalence partitioning and boundary value analysis, we prepared a discrete data domain which is an equivalent representation of the complete and continuous original data domain. We now aim at the identification of an incomplete set of branch-free critical sequences through this abstracted, discrete domain model.

At the core is the reduction of the process domain. The approach is a double reduction: first, transformation and block building on process scheme level, and then numerical (de-)selection on the level of process instances (or, test sequences) in the simplified scheme. In this way, we deliberately resign from completeness twice. In other words, we first select the critical scheme parts from the overall process flow that need testing coverage. This leads to a simplified process scheme. The selected scheme parts that are deemed critical by the customer are at the same time numerically unfolded according to the abstracted domain model (i.e. all possible "traces" are listed that can be derived from the business rules). Now we can select a small number out of all possible numerical sequences through this simplified domain process scheme. The result is a small critical subset out of the very large set of all possible paths through the abstracted domain model.

Criteria to be used are based on aware stakeholder priority decisions, e.g. on business criticality of different process scheme parts and of different "traces" through the simplified model. This could be measured e.g. in terms of monetary value flow per path. If e.g. in a process scheme half of the revenues are generated within a certain small subset of maybe ten percent of the full scheme, and the other half of the revenue generation happens throughout the remaining ninety percent of the scheme, then apparently the smaller subset of the scheme is probably more important for the end-user testing. In this simplified example we could even already calculate a very simple priority value from the figures. The further elaboration of underlying stakeholder criteria would lead away from the scope of this paper. At this point we just need to take the diligent assumption that we are able to prioritize process scheme parts and process instances according to their business value.

From computability theory we can derive the fundamental process flow constructs "sequence", "join" and "split" selection (joining pre-conditions, splitting post-conditions, also known as "selection") and "iteration", which are also described and used as starting point for workflow patterns definitions (van der Aalst et al. 2003). Process flow patterns use constructs ranging from these simple elements up to complex processing primitives. For each of the three basic constructs, we take workflow patterns from van der Aalst et al. (2003) and show how transformation and block building works for the basic construct; the notation used in the figures is UML activity diagram (Object Management Group 2005). The full domain process flow can then be treated iteratively by treating the single basic constructs.

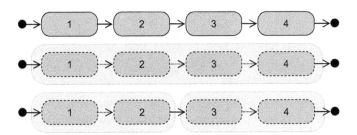

Figure IV.R6-3: Sequence blocking.

A *sequence* of process steps as shown in Figure IV.R6-3 is found in the basic workflow pattern "sequence". It reflects the fundamental notion of an activity that is enabled after the completion of the preceding activity, and a common interpretation for the pattern is implication or causality.

As a linear sequence this basic construct is already in the form of our intended result, and we can – without further transformation – readily form a block unit by using any continuous subsequence of it; in Figure IV.R6-3, the second line shows a block built from the maximum subsequence, the third line shows an alternative block building. Each block can then be (de-)selected as a whole unit. This means that numerical test, and as a consequence also oracles, will be set at the block boundaries only; in line three of Figure IV.R6-3 before activity 1 and after activity 2, and before activity 3 and after activity 4, but not, say, after activity 1. This implies that even when including the block unit, there will be no consideration of block internals. In the reduced, simplified process scheme, the internal structure of the block is hidden.

A *split* selection of the activities flow into multiple activities as shown in Figure IV.R6-4 is found in the basic workflow patterns "XOR-split" and "AND-split". The patterns reflect the essential notion of branching activities. A common interpretation for the XOR-split or switch pattern shown on the upper left side of the figure is decision. A common interpretation for the AND-split or fork pattern shown on the upper right side of the figure is parallel processing.

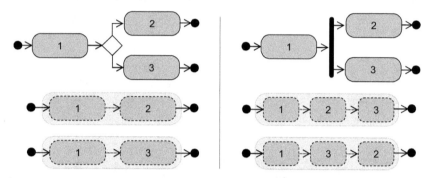

Figure IV.R6-4: Split transformation and blocking.

For both split types, we transform the process scheme into a simpler scheme for blocking as shown in Figure IV.R6-4. On a binary XOR switch, as well as on a binary AND fork, two blocks encompass the construct, one block for each of the two subsequent steps within the scheme part. Splits with more than two following steps can be handled accordingly and result in more than two blocks. The internal block structures become hidden on the simplified scheme level. Numerical selection of the single "traces" in a subsequent step is less complex and establishes linear paths. Note that the concurrency aspect of the AND-split disappears, which seems appropriate for the intended testing against reuse specifications and without executable software.

A *join* selection of the activities flow from multiple activities as shown in Figure IV.R6-5 is found in the basic workflow patterns "XOR-join" and "AND-join". It reflects the essential notion of merging activities. A common interpretation for the XOR-join pattern shown on the upper left side of the figure is trigger. A common interpretation for the AND-join pattern shown on the upper right side of the figure is synchronization.

For both join types, we transform the process scheme into a simpler scheme for blocking as shown in Figure IV.R6-5. On a binary XOR trigger, as well as on a binary AND synchronization, two blocks encompass the whole construct, one block for each of the two preceding steps within the scheme constructs. Joins with more than two preceding steps can be handled accordingly and lead to more than two blocks. Again the internal block structures become hidden to the unfolding in the numerical reduction, when we select the "traces" in a subsequent step. Note also here that the synchronization aspect of the AND-join disappears, which again seems appropriate for the intended testing against reuse specifications and without executable software.

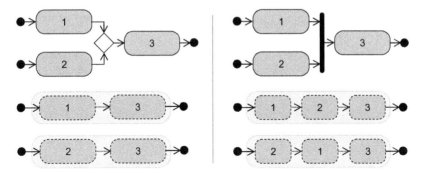

Figure IV.R6-5: Join transformation and blocking.

An *iteration* in the activities flow as shown in Figure IV.R6-6 is found in the structural workflow pattern "arbitrary cycles". It reflects the notion of activities that can be done repeatedly. A common interpretation for repeated activities patterns is loop.

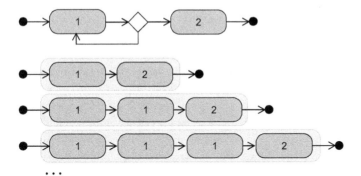

Figure IV.R6-6: Iteration transformation and blocking.

For an iteration construct in a real workflow, we transform the process scheme into a simpler scheme for blocking. We use the same approach as with the other constructs and unfold the iteration primitive into single linear paths. The number of possible paths is determined by the business rules ("loop conditions"). The number can be large, even in a non-theoretical workflow, even with an abstracted data domain and single value representatives per equivalence class (as produced from the preceding abstraction step).

Our approach is to bundle equivalence classes for iterations so that as many "traces" through the loop as possible fall into the same equivalence category. We start at the general and known approach to leave out sub-paths from the transformed iteration that are passed more than k times. We argue for our validation purposes that a sub-path that is included in a related larger path needs to be looked at only once, and so we set $k = 1$ (the example given later demonstrates the application of the idea). Together with the iterative sequence blocking in our approach, we still have the possibility to explicitly include also sub-paths that were identified as business critical within the loop, if they are included in a larger path (as suggested in the second and third line in Figure IV.R6-6). So we established a basis for selecting the critical passes that are needed for inclusion as validation scenarios.

Note that for our higher-order testing of reuse specifications we can omit unsolvable cases from information theory (cf. e.g. halting problem).

With the transformation and blocking procedures we can construct paths through the abstracted domain that are (i) part of the domain under consideration, (ii) critical for the customer and (iii) linear, without branches and without cycles. We call such a path a "Sunshine Path". Sunshine Paths can be serialized by construction, because they are a linear sequence of process steps, or transactions, which produce the same result as in the originating graph, if they were completely selected. They now go into the inclusion step as building blocks for end-to-end validation scenarios.

3.3   Example

The example is non-fictitious on the domain side and is taken from a large company's business rules and processes for the creation of credit items. Figure IV.R6-7 shows one function out of the process diagram and the relevant business rules for the "authorization level ok?" process step. A credit item has been recorded by an agent of the company at this stage. Now it needs formal release. Everyone involved in the process belongs unambiguously to a certain role, and all roles have limits for releasing (rel) a recorded credit item depending on its amount. If the credit amount is above the role's limit, it is not released by the role but instead submitted (sub) to the next superior role. Above a certain amount, any credit needs release by two different authorized roles (rel-s, rel). The two highest roles are entitled to release all credits. In the described process, credits that shall not be released remain in an undefined, or submitted, state.

Abstraction maps the original domain model onto an equivalent domain model with defined discrete partitions and distinct value representatives per partition. The example results in seven partitions shown in Table IV.R6-1 together with their values. If the analyzed customer domain section does not define any observable behavior, e.g. for partition P_1 in this example, then tests cannot be derived from this part of the domain model.

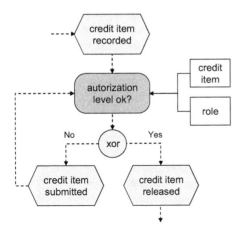

ROLE	THRESHOLD (EUR)
CC	< 50.-
CR	< 250.-
Regional Coordinator	< 1'000.-
Admin Credit Dept.	< 1'000.-
Manager BU	< 5'000.-
Manager MS	>= 1'000.- and < 5'000.-
Director F	>= 5'000.-
Director S	>= 5'000.-

A credit item is released if its net amount is below the authorization threshold of the role. Credit items above limits are submitted to the next superior role. In regions without Regional Coordinator, an Admin Credit Dept. from the head quarter steps in. Starting from 500.- credit items need release from two authorized roles.

Figure IV.R6-7: Domain model excerpt.

Further simplification of the scheme and its business rules by transformation and blocking is not necessary in the simple example. Reduction can readily identify the "traces" or, data sequences that are critical and reasonable for testing from the full set of possible sequences, from an end-user validation point of view.

Partition	Value		Partition	Value
$P_1 =]-\infty; 0]$	$e_1 = -1$		$P_5 = [500; 1000[$	$e_5 = 500$
$P_2 = [0; 50[$	$e_2 = 25$		$P_6 = [1000; 5000[$	$e_6 = 1000$
$P_3 = [50; 250[$	$e_3 = 50$		$P_7 = [5000; \infty[$	$e_7 = 5000$
$P_4 = [250; 500[$	$e_4 = 250$			

Table IV.R6-1: Partitions and values.

We restrict to demonstrating positive test sequences here, negative test sequences work according to the same principle. The iteration on the example can be reduced from an end-user's business perspective to sequences starting at the least empowered call center (cc) role, which will subsequently cover also superior roles with suitable partition values (i.e. no explicit check for $k > 1$ in a first approach).

This reduction results in Table IV.R6-2 listing ten Sunshine Path sequences, the building blocks for critical business scenarios through the domain section. These sequences are now eligible for inclusion, also with critical sequences from other, interconnected domain parts, to build end-to-end branch-free business scenarios. The approach to connect sequences is the same as it was shown for the steps within a domain part. Joining two scenarios becomes possible by using the preceding scenario's output as the subsequent scenario's input. Inclusion criteria, again, are fully domain centric.

Role	cca	cr	rc	acd	mbu	mms	df	ds
S_1	e_2 rel	-	-	-	-	-	-	-
S_2	e_3 sub	e_3 rel	-	-	-	-	-	-
S_3	e_4 sub	e_4 sub	e_4 rel	-	-	-	-	-
S_4	e_4 sub	e_4 sub	-	e_4 rel	-	-	-	-
S_5	e_5 sub	e_5 sub	e_5 rel-s	-	e_5 rel	-	-	-
S_6	e_5 sub	e_5 sub	-	e_5 rel-s	e_5 rel	-	-	-
S_7	e_6 sub	e_6 sub	e_6 sub	-	e_6 rel-s	e_6 rel	-	-
S_8	e_6 sub	e_6 sub	-	e_6 sub	e_6 rel-s	e_6 rel	-	-
S_9	e_7 sub	e_7 sub	e_7 sub	-	e_7 sub	-	e_7 rel-s	e_7 rel
S_{10}	e_7 sub	e_7 sub	-	e_7 sub	e_7 sub	-	e_7 rel-s	e_7 rel

Table IV.R6-2: "Sunshine path" sequences.

To demonstrate how we check a specification artifact on the basis of the sequences from Table IV.R6-2, it is assumed that a software provider has specified and offered a fictitious Comparator software component. Next to other levels and facts, the behavior of this software artifact is described in OCL (Object Constraint Language) from Object Management Group (2006), and a checkGE service ("greater or equal") is defined according to Figure IV.R6-8. It is also specified for the Comparator component, on the respective layer of a multi-level reuse specification, that a limits relation maps a value to an actor.

```
context comparator::checkGE( val:Real, act:String ):Boolean
pre:
        ( oclIsUndefined( val )=false )
        and
        ( oclIsUndefined( act )=false )
        and
        self.limits->exists( actor:String | actor=act )
post:
        if self.limits->select( actor:String | acor:act ).value >= val
        then result=true  -- greater or equal
        else result=false - not (greater or equal)
        endif
```

Figure IV.R6-8: Behavioral specification artifact (OCL).

To check the behavior specified in Figure IV.R6-8 against customer requirements given as critical sequences, the constraints from the supplier's specification are now numerically compared with one ore more branch-free scenarios. As described, such a scenario can be one path through several subsequent critical customer sequences from interrelated domain parts that are assembled and validated together.

We assume in this example that our customer includes one single Sunshine Path, S_4 from Table IV.R6-2. So we can restrict our example to demonstrate this single sequence. In natural language, S_4 follows a recorded credit item of 250.– from a region without regional coordinator role. The credit item is (i) beyond the credit authorization limit of the call center role and therefore submitted to the customer representative role. It is (ii) beyond the credit authorization limit of the customer representative role and therefore submitted to the administrator credit department role. It is (iii) within the credit authorization limit of the administrator credit department role and released. Validation of this sequence is done by systematically walking through the OCL constraints from Figure IV.R6-8.

In step (i) the first two preconditions hold: `val` is 250.– and `act` is cca. The third precondition also holds: once the mapping table is set up with role descriptions and thresholds from the domain model, then cca will be found in the `limits` relation. If the preconditions hold as described, the specification's postcondition will evaluate (50 >= 250) and return false. The work flow can identify this with the meaning that the credit item is not released, and return to the "authorization level ok?" function with a "credit item submitted" state.

In step (ii) the first two preconditions hold: `val` is 250 and `act` is cr. As in the previous step the third precondition also holds for cr. If the preconditions hold as described, the specification's postcondition will evaluate (250 >= 250) and return true. The work flow can identify this with the meaning that the credit item is released, and continue to further parts of the domain model with a "credit item released" state.

In step (iii) the first two preconditions hold: `val` is 250 and `act` is acd. As in the previous steps the third precondition also holds for acd. If the preconditions hold as described, the specification's postcondition will evaluate (1000 >= 250) and return true. The work flow can identify this with the meaning that the credit item is released, and continue to further parts of the domain model with a "credit item released" state.

Thus, on the bottom line, validation of the `Comparator` component vs. S_4 using ARIval revealed a problem. While steps (i) and (iii) can be performed correctly by the specified software, in step (ii) the `Comparator` component fails check vs. the business rules. In the domain model and its critical sequence S_4, the credit item of 250.– is not released by a customer representative but instead submitted to be checked by the superior role. In the `Comparator` component, the validation shows that the credit item of 250.– is actually released by the customer representative role, which is inconsistent with the requirements from the domain model.

Possible consequences of this result could include looking for a `checkG` service ("greater") of the `Comparator` component, or changing the business rules slightly, or others. In any case the small but on the domain side non-fictitious validation example has shown that the proposed method gives an early hint at the necessity of a respective, aware decision and provides tangible support for it, without using any actual software.

4   Related work

Component software testing theory has become a large area of scientific research (Vincenzi et al. 2003). Important existing approaches with relation to our method have been selected and are shown in Table IV.R6-3 to demarcate original contributions of the method.

Approach	Component (Program) verification	Composition (Architecture) ver. & val.	Context (Domain) validation
Built-in test technology	X		
Formal methods	X	(X)	
Scenario-/model-based testing	(X)	(X)	(X)
Specification matching	X		X
Tabular notation	X		
Test / composition languages	(X)	X	
Test input data sampling	X	(X)	
Test output oracles	X		
This approach (ARIval)		(X)	X

Table IV.R6-3: Related approaches.

Lines in Table IV.R6-3 list the examined approaches which are further described below. Columns list three abstraction levels: component, composition and context. On component level formal program verification of single components with their interfaces is typical research focus. On composition level research from formal and less formal areas deals with architectures of several integrated components. On context level research focus is on the requirements side and less formal, concerned with system architectures in their socio-technical domain and business context. The availability of an approach for different abstraction levels is indicated in the cells. Our method's research contributions on the domain level or context level are: embedding into a clear business model, independent domain based test oracles, and early domain level testing before software is available. The analyzed existing approaches don't seem to cover this.

Built-in test technologies. Built-in technologies for self-testing software components, in analogy to built-in tests from integrated circuits, have extensively been researched, e.g. in the Component+ project of the European Union (Edler & Hörnstein 2003). Built-in tests come within the component, e.g. as additional test services, and are not intended to represent independent customer specific automation requirements but basic technical checks. Tests built into the component by their vendors are complementary to our domain centric axiom.

Formal methods. Especially in formal model checking, plenty of verification approaches ("are we building the software right?") are discussed, among them the interesting domain reduction abstraction (Choi & Heimdahl 2003). The method proposed here transfers some of the ideas to the domain validation ("are we building the right software?") viewpoint. But fully formal approaches for real components are prevented by computational effort with real systems in practice, decidability problems from computer theory, the absence of complete formal specifications, and the lack of a justifying business case or public interest. Also, formal verification can still be wrong. Formal verification methods provide valuable insight but in a practical sense don't apply to our complex domain level validation.

Scenario based and model based testing. Scenarios can be seen as special entities within the more general notion of a model. In model based testing, test references are generated from a model of the actual system. Many model based test approaches build upon the UML (Unified Modeling Language) today, and derive test references from UML diagrams (Offutt & Abdurazik 1999; Briand & Labiche 2002). Test references in existing approaches are built from artifacts within the component software development – models, design scenarios, etc. – and not from independent and unknown customer requirements as proposed here. Few if any approaches have yet addressed these model independency issues and its test implications, as does our method on the domain validation side.

Specification matching. Existing approaches are based on fully formal language specifications, focus strongly on technical aspects, and are restricted to the matching of relatively simple functions (Moormann Zaremski & Wing 1997; Yellin & Strom 1997). Semi-formal matching methods from library science have also been described since long (Prieto-Díaz & Freeman 1987; Penix & Alexander 1999), and discussions exist to automatically extract classification attributes from natural language descriptions (Maarek, Berry & Kaiser 1991). Further investigations include in particular relaxations of exact matching, and also contextual refinement theory (Fidge 2002). Discussions started only recently that focus on more complex business domain perspectives for compatibility considerations of multi-layered specifications (Zaha 2004). Our method goes beyond formal technical aspects and aims at checking specifications vs. higher-order requirements represented by domain level scenarios.

Tabular notation. This approach aims at representing requirements fully formal by using a comprehensible, mathematically precise tabular notation of predicate logic for partial functions (Parnas 1993). Domain requirements are successively translated into this tabular form, with promising first practical results (Baber et al. 2005). Tabular notation seems very formal for "good enough" testing as intended in our method.

Test and composition languages. Similar to well known specification languages such as Z or OCL, special languages for testing and for composition have been proposed. One example on the testing side is TTCN-3 for test execution (Grabowski et al. 2003). An example on the composition side is the Piccola calculus for formal component composition (Achermann & Nierstrasz 2005). Test languages make implicit assumptions on their domains and their intended use, and have proven successful for testing software in their respective target areas. Architectural composition languages are formal and powerful but don't seem suitable for defining and evaluating actual test scenarios. Our method suggests a generic, widely applicable domain validation method without actual software but based on reuse specifications.

Test input data sampling. Exhaustive testing on all possible inputs is infeasible in general and inappropriate in particular for large real life enterprise applications. Hence an incomplete but appropriate test has to be determined. Existing approaches achieve this by sampling a domain of the input data according to fault hypotheses i.e. assumptions about which aspects or entities are error prone, allowing the test to reveal as many failures as possible with a minimum effort (Beizer 1995). In our method, tests are generated not from fault hypotheses within the technological software system or its specification or models, but instead independently from the actual customer's ontological domain and its automation requirements which are unknown to, and detached from, the component software technology provider.

Test output oracles. The test oracle question (Turing 1939; Weyuker 1982) relates to outputs produced by a test: if the actual results differ from the expected results, did a proper test run produce wrong results revealing a software error, or were the expected results and/or the testing and/or basic assumptions wrong in the first place? Particular test outputs need careful analysis if the oracle grounds on the same model as the software (Pretschner & Philipps 2005). Related issues can be observed in the controversial discussions of N-version programming in the 1980s. Sophisticated approaches such as e.g. (Hummel & Atkinson 2005) exist today. Our method instead sets priority to tests created independently from a software user, to deliver the independent oracle and the final judgment about an expected feature of a reused component.

5   Summary and conclusions

Compositional reuse for industry style software production is an important approach pursued to master the ever increasing demands on software intensive systems. Testing black box software components from large repositories for their suitability to be reused in an actual end-user situation is among the problems that complicate this approach. The associated validation activities are supported by the ARIval method, offering to the component demand side a domain centric component validation approach. The approach has some core advantages: it is derived from a clear business model assumption, sources test oracles from business domain requirements independent from the technological development process, and produces tangible results early, before the executable software is available, on the basis of suppliers' reuse specifications.

We demonstrated the principle in an example which is non-fictitious on the domain side. By constructing critical scenarios via abstraction, reduction and inclusion from a domain model, we obtain branch-free Sunshine Paths of automation sequences deemed validation critical on the domain level of the demand side. These scenarios represent references against which relevant levels from multi-dimensional supplier black box specifications can be checked very early in the compositional development process, and with oracles that are independent from this development process.

With our approach we support early and independent higher-order black box component software testing on the demand side in industrialized software processes. This can benefit software component customers through earlier and better testing within further decomposed division of work as required for industrialized software engineering processes.

References

Achermann, F.; Nierstrasz, O. (2005), "A calculus for reasoning about software composition", *Theoretical Computer Science*, 331 (2-3): 367-396.

Ackermann, J.; Brinkop, F.; Conrad, S.; Fettke, P.; Frick, A.; Glistau, E.; Jaekel, H.; Kotlar, O.; Loos, P.; Mrech, H.; Ortner, E.; Raape, U.; Overhage, S.; Sahm, S.; Schmietendorf, A.; Teschke, T.; Turowski, K. (2002), "Standardized Specification of Business Components", Gesellschaft für Informatik, Augsburg.

Baber, R.; Parnas, D.; Vilkomir, S.; Harrison, P.; O'Connor, T. (2005), "Disciplined methods of software specification: A case study", *Proceedings of the international symposium on information technology: Coding and computing*, IEEE Computer Society, 4-6 Apr. 2006, Las Vegas, USA: 428-437.

Beizer, B. (1995), *Black-box testing: Techniques for functional testing of software and systems*, Wiley, New York, USA.

Biggerstaff, T.; Richter, C. (1987), "Reusability framework, assessment, and directions", *IEEE Software*, 4 (2): 41-49.

Boehm, B. (2005), "The future of software processes", *Unifying the software process spectrum: Proceedings of the international software process workshop: Revised selected papers*, Lecture Notes in Computer Science 3840, Springer, 25-27 May 2005, Beijing, China: 10-24.

Briand, L.; Labiche, Y. (2002), "A UML-based approach to system testing", *Journal of Software and Systems Modeling*, 1 (1): 10-42.

Brooks, F. (1987), "No silver bullet: Essence and accidents of software engineering", *IEEE Computer*, 20 (4): 10-19.

Choi, Y.; Heimdahl, M. (2003), "Model checking software requirement specifications using domain reduction abstraction", *Proceedings of the 18th IEEE international conference on automated software engineering*, IEEE Computer Society, 6-10 Oct. 2003, Montreal, Canada: 314-317.

Dietz, J. (2006), *Enterprise ontology: Theory and methodology*, Springer, Berlin.

Edler, H.; Hörnstein, J. (2003), Component+ final report 1.1., accessed on 12 Oct. 2005, http://www.component-plus.org/pdf/reports/Final report 1.1.pdf.

Fidge, C. (2002), "Contextual matching of software library components", *Proceedings of the 9th Asia-Pacific software engineering conference*, IEEE Computer Society, 4-6 Dec. 2002, Gold Coast, Australia: 297-306.

Gao, J.; Tsao, H.; Wu, Y. (2003), *Testing and quality assurance for component-based software*, Artech House, Boston, USA.

Gordijn, J.; Akkermans, H. (2001), "Designing and evaluating e-business models", *IEEE Intelligent Systems*, 16 (4): 11-17.

Grabowski, J.; Hogrefe, D.; Réthy, G.; Schieferdecker, I.; Wiles, A.; Willcock, C. (2003), "An introduction to the testing and test control notation (TTCN-3)", *Computer Networks*, 42 (3): 375-403.

Hummel, O.; Atkinson, C. (2005), "Automated harvesting of test oracles for reliability testing", *Proceedings of the 29th annual international computer software and applications conference*, IEEE Computer Society, 25-28 Jul. 2005, Edinburgh, UK: 196-202.

Maarek, Y.; Berry, D.; Kaiser, G. (1991), "An information retrieval approach for automatically constructing software libraries", *IEEE Transactions on Software Engineering*, 17 (8): 800-813.

McIlroy, M. (1969), "Mass produced software components", *Software engineering: Report on a conference sponsored by the NATO Science Committee*, NATO Scientific Affairs Division, 7-11 Oct. 1968, Garmisch: 138-155.

Meyer, B. (1992), "Applying 'design by contract'", *IEEE Computer*, 25 (10): 40-51.

Meyer, B. (2003), "The grand challenge of trusted components", *Proceedings of the 25th international conference on software engineering*, IEEE Computer Society, 3-10 May 2003, Portland, USA: 660-667.

Mili, H.; Mili, F.; Mili, A. (1995), "Reusing software: Issues and research directions", *IEEE Transactions on Software Engineering*, 21 (6): 528-562.

Moormann Zaremski, A.; Wing, J. (1997), "Specification matching of software components", *ACM Transactions on Software Engineering and Methodology*, 6 (4): 333-369.

Myers, G. (1979), *The art of software testing*, Wiley, New York, USA.

Object Management Group (2005), Unified modeling language: Superstructure version 2.0, accessed on 31 Mar. 2006, http://www.omg.org/docs/formal/05-07-04.pdf.

Object Management Group (2006), UML 2.0. OCL specification, accessed on 24 Oct. 2006, http://www.omg. org/cgi-bin/apps/doc?formal/06-05-01.pdf.

Offutt, J.; Abdurazik, A. (1999), "Generating tests from UML specifications", *The Unified Modeling Language – Beyond the Standard: Proceedings of the 2nd International Conference*, Lecture Notes in Computer Science 1723, Springer, 28-30 Oct. 1999, Fort Collins, USA: 416-429.

Overhage, S. (2006), "Vereinheitlichte Spezifikation von Komponenten: Grundlagen, UnSCom Spezifikationsrahmen und Anwendung", Dissertation, Universität Augsburg, Augsburg.

Parnas, D. (1993), "Predicate logic for software engineering", *IEEE Transactions on Software Engineering*, 19 (9): 856-862.

Parnas, D. (2001), "Software aspects of strategic defense systems", in Hoffman, D.; Weiss, D. (eds), *Software fundamentals: Collected papers by David L. Parnas*, Addison Wesley, Boston, USA: 497-518.

Penix, J.; Alexander, P. (1999), "Efficient specification-based component retrieval", *Automated Software Engineering*, 6 (2): 139-170.

Pretschner, A.; Philipps, J. (2005), "Methodological issues in model-based testing", in Broy, M.; Jonsson, B.; Katoen, J.; Leucker, M.; Pretschner, A. (eds), *Model-based testing of reactive systems: Advanced lectures*, Lecture Notes in Computer Science 3472, Springer, Berlin: 281-291.

Prieto-Díaz, R.; Freeman, P. (1987), "Classifying software for reusability", *IEEE Software*, 4 (1): 6-16.

Skroch, O. (2007), "Validation of component-based software with a customer centric domain level approach", *Proceedings of the 14th annual IEEE international conference and workshop on the engineering of computer based systems*, IEEE Computer Society, 26-29 Mar. 2007, Tucson, USA: 459-466.

Szyperski, C.; Gruntz, D.; Murer, S. (2002), *Component software: Beyond object-oriented programming*, 2nd edn, Addison Wesley, London, UK.

Turing, A. (1939), "Systems of logic based on ordinals", *Proceedings of the London Mathematical Society*, s2-45 (1): 161-228.

Turowski, K. (2003), *Fachkomponenten: Komponentenbasierte betriebliche Anwendungssysteme*, Shaker, Aachen.

van der Aalst, W.; ter Hofstede, A.; Kiepuszewski, B.; Barros, A. (2003), "Workflow patterns", *Distributed and Parallel Databases*, 14 (1): 5-51.

Vincenzi, A.; Maldonado, J.; Delamaro, M.; Spoto, E.; Wong, W. (2003), "Component-based software: An overview of testing", in Cechich, A.; Piattini, M.; Vallecillo, A. (eds), *Component-based software quality: Methods and techniques*, Lecture Notes in Computer Science 2693, Springer, Berlin: 99-127.

Weyuker, E. (1982), "On testing non-testable programs", *The Computer Journal*, 25 (4): 465-470.

Weyuker, E. (1998), "Testing component-based software: A cautionary tale", *IEEE Software*, 15 (5): 54-59.

Yellin, D.; Strom, R. (1997), "Protocol specifications and component adaptors", *ACM Transactions on Programming Languages and Systems*, 19 (2): 292-333.

Yourdon, E. (1995), "When good enough software is best", *IEEE Software*, 12 (3): 79-81.

Zaha, J. (2004), "Automated compatibility tests for business related aspects of software components", *On the move to meaningful Internet systems: Workshop proceedings*, Lecture Notes in Computer Science 3292, Springer, 25-29 October 2004, Agia Napa, Cyprus: 834-841.

V   Conclusions and outlook

V.1   Conclusions

The research articles presented in this book have discussed business informatics issues within the component- and service-oriented mission statement for the development of application software systems (Turowski 2003, pp. 9-15). The main topic was the arrangement of application software development from different perspectives. Aiming at an end-to-end consideration within the framework of strategic software reuse (long-term), the articles covered different aspects of the specification (tactical) and the selection (operational) of components and services.

The first two articles dealt with basic strategic conditions of software reuse, both starting from the multi-path process model (Ortner 1998, p. 332; Overhage 2006, p. 136).

In research article R1, two basic software reuse strategies could be distinguished, compositional and generative reuse. Also, two ideal type market environments could be described, stable markets of the "old economy" and turbulent "high-tech" market conditions. Supported by the analysis of experiences from three development projects with software reuse included, a new theory for preferences of reuse approaches according to market environments could be built. Two concrete and justified hypotheses were formulated and can be checked empirically. So the research objectives could be reached. To enable the formulation of the hypotheses, a "reductionist" approach was taken and narrowing assumptions were made. The described market conditions are quite idealized, as well as the strategic decision alternatives assumed by the theory. The strategies are related to one single market environment and not to several different environments and influences at the same time. Further factors other than market conditions also have an impact on software reuse approaches. While reasonable hypotheses were built, they do not serve as a strategic software reuse guideline yet, but as an initial step towards the rational identification of strategic preferences for reuse principles in relation to prevalent market environments.

In research article R2, the well-known "make-or-buy" issue in software development was examined in a large reference project. In literature, projects of this kind and size have rarely been examined and described so close to reality. In the reference project, it was analyzed in detail how well requirements for a complex, intra- and inter-organizational application system are covered by an individually developed solution. In a second step, and on the same level of detail, this was compared to the requirements coverage achieved by a combination of commercial software packages offered for reuse and integration on the market. Experiences from other large projects with similarities to the reference project were examined additionally. The comparison of requirements coverage between the two different development strategies in the reference project favored the reuse and integration approach. The examination of further projects did not convey an unambiguous picture though. Hence the research objectives could partly be reached. The findings suggest that there are other critical success factors apart from the question of development or procurement. The self-evident option of a combined "make-*and*-buy" strategy could not be examined either, since the regarded projects were planned and operated without this alternative. Finally, it is unlikely that the examined projects constitute a fully representative sample.

Two articles on tactical aspects were concentrated on specification as a particularly challenging task which at the same time is maybe the single most important part in the component- and service-oriented software development cycle (Alpar et al. 2008, p. 294; Sommerville 2001, p. 107).

Research article R3 illustrated the central role of requirements specifications and the derived scope of work descriptions for the daily practice of divided software development work. Critical success factors were then identified which promote the practical creation of high quality requirements specifications. Moreover, risks were figured out that can arise from unclear scope of work descriptions, including the most unfavorable outcome, a legal dispute. This assertively interdisciplinary notion at the interface between business informatics and law is a novelty, and the research objectives could be reached. The findings, however, are based on the valuations and opinions of few experts who are very experienced both on the theoretical side and in practice.

Research article R4 presented a method proposing an approach for the systematic evaluation of the suitability of requirements specifications in downstream offshore development steps and its application in a large case study. The practical applicability of the proposed approach was demonstrated by its smooth execution in the real industry context of the study. The evaluations and predictions from the approach were validated against the actual further course of the development project in the studied case. So one step was made towards a new, systematic method for respective planning and decision support based on requirements specifications in offshore development situations, and the research objectives could be reached. The empirical confirmation rests upon a single case study. The studied case was large, real, and relevant, and it is straightforward to apply the proposed approach in further case studies and projects. The universal validity of the approach has not yet been confirmed though.

The final two articles were concerned with the operational choice of services, as seen from the demand perspective within the mission statement of the component- and service-oriented development of application software systems (Turowski 2003, pp. 9-15).

In research article R5, the characteristics of an opportunistic ad hoc search for suitable and eligible (Web-)services on the Internet were determined. A method was proposed to improve this search and the related service selection. Results from theories of optimal stopping in mathematical statistics were applied in two scenarios for self-adapting service-oriented systems. Stopping algorithms which correspond to the application scenarios were deduced and implemented. In simulation experiments, the operational advantages of an open, dynamic system with service selection strategies supported from optimal stopping were measured and confirmed against a closed, static system. So the research objectives could be reached. A basic assumption is the availability of several functionally equivalent services on the Internet, all of them eligible to perform a certain subtask within a component- and service-oriented overall system; not all experts share this assumption today. The method also implements improvements to a process which needs to consider semantic and pragmatic criteria for search and selection. While the underlying issues are among the intensely discussed research questions, no final or satisfactory solution has been found by now.

In research article R6, a method was proposed to decompose business processes into single non-branching scenarios, to use the linear scenarios as skeletons for the definition of end-to-end test scenarios; and to check the operational suitability of reusable components and services based on their specifications against the scenarios. An example was presented where an actual EPC excerpt is reduced to linear scenarios, which are converted into independent test oracles and used as a reference to check an OCL specification artifact. This early "higher-order" testing with oracles that are independent from the development process is an important and often neglected advantage. The possibility to quantify test coverage measures from the set of linear end-to-end scenarios is another. So the research objectives could partly be reached. Limitations include the systematic reduction of business process models to non-branching scenarios, which depends on the language used for the business process model. Using specifications as independent test oracles also depends on the degree of formality and the detail level of the specification. The universal applicability of the method has not been finally discussed.

In summary, the main part of this book presented research results in six articles on the specification and selection of components and services within the strategic, long-term approach of reuse-driven development for component- and service-oriented application software systems.

V.2   Outlook

Four from six research articles presented in the main part of this book have reached their research objectives, the other two research articles (R2, R6) have reached them at least partly. Interesting future research can tie in with the findings from each research article.

In research article R1, two hypotheses on strategic software reuse preferences in relation to market conditions have been built. Future research could further refine and advance these hypotheses. Finally, the hypotheses will need an empirical examination, which might be difficult to perform though.

In research article R2, strategic advantages of software reuse, as compared to individually developed software, could be confirmed by means of the detailed examination of a large reference project. The analysis of further projects bearing similarities to this reference project did not clearly direct for or against software reuse any more. Future research could tie in with this second finding and, for instance, aim at isolating other critical success factors that have not been identified.

In research article R3, the importance of requirements specifications in divided software development work was illustrated. Critical success factors for creating requirements specifications were highlighted. Risks from neglecting them were portrayed, with a specific focus on interdisciplinary risks at the interface between business informatics and law. The article is based on valuations and opinions of experts. Future research could complement the findings with an analysis of related literature. The outstanding significance of requirements specifications in two topical research directions – component- and service-oriented software and offshore software development – could also be examined more deeply in this context.

In research article R4, a large requirements specification was examined in a case study by applying a theoretically well-founded method proposed to evaluate a specification's suitability in an offshore development situation. The case study was performed in an industry context and yielded positive research results. Interesting future research can tie in with these results in several directions. One possible research direction is to provide further empirical checks by applying the method in a controlled way in other practical cases and, when indicated, adjust the method accordingly. Another possible research direction is to further advance and refine the method analytically, e.g. by providing a fully formal description.

In research article R5, the dynamic search and selection of appropriate (Web-)services on the Internet was improved in two scenarios by deducing and applying algorithms from optimal stopping theories. Assumptions include stable requirements and the opportunistic search for the best possible service. Without loss of generality, service discovery events were assumed to be uniformly distributed. Future research could work on the determination of empirical distribution functions. The method could also be examined for its applicability in situations with several optimization criteria and goal conflicts, such as service quality against costs of service invocation. Another interesting future research direction would be to extend the method and make it applicable to systems that dynamically adapt to functionally instable requirements. Future research could benefit from the simulation components which were implemented for this research and which are easily adaptable, effective, and reusable.

In research article R6, non-branching paths were extracted from a business process model, end-to-end test scenarios were defined from these paths, and specifications of reusable software components were checked against these scenarios. Interesting research questions can be derived from these results. Future research could aim at identifying the preconditions to be met so that a business process model can be reduced to linear paths in the sense of the method. Theoretical barriers, for instance, from computational complexity, should then be considered together with pragmatic assumptions and empirical investigations about sizes and types of business process models that actually exist. Future research could also describe in more detail how linear paths through a business process model can be transformed to end-to-end test scenarios, including in particular the definition and generation of test data. Future research could also aim at defining the preconditions that must be met by specifications before they can serve as test oracles. Finally, the definition of metrics to measure the coverage of "higher-order" tests is also an interesting research direction with major practical relevance.

Beyond future research demands that directly tie in with the individual articles that were presented in the main part of this book, it can be stated that the creative exercise of application software development in component- and service-oriented concepts has by far not been examined completely yet. As it was demonstrated also in this book, it is a research direction which stipulates warrantable expectations for findings and advances that strengthen competitiveness in practice and help to sustain a scientifically challenging and prolific field of research within business informatics also in the future.

References

Alpar, P.; Grob, H.; Weimann, P.; Winter, R. (2008), *Anwendungsorientierte Wirtschaftsinformatik: Strategische Planung, Entwicklung und Nutzung von Informations- und Kommunikationssystemen*, 5th edn, Vieweg, Wiesbaden.

Ortner, E. (1998), "Ein Multipfad-Vorgehensmodell für die Entwicklung von Informationssystemen – dargestellt am Beispiel von Workflow-Management Anwendungen", *Wirtschaftsinformatik*, 40 (4): 329-337.

Overhage, S. (2006), "Vereinheitlichte Spezifikation von Komponenten: Grundlagen, UnSCom Spezifikationsrahmen und Anwendung", Dissertation, Universität Augsburg, Augsburg.

Sommerville, I. (2001), *Software engineering*, 6th edn, Pearson, Munich.

Turowski, K. (2003), *Fachkomponenten: Komponentenbasierte betriebliche Anwendungssysteme*, Shaker, Aachen.

www.ingramcontent.com/pod-product-compliance
Lightning Source LLC
La Vergne TN
LVHW052301060326
832902LV00021B/3649